Fix It!™ Grammar

Town Mouse and Country Mouse

TEACHER'S MANUAL
LEVEL 2

Pamela White

Fourth Edition, January 2022
Institute for Excellence in Writing, L.L.C.

The purchase of this book allows its owner access to e-audio resource talks by Andrew Pudewa. See blue page for details and download instructions.

ISBN 978-1-62341-360-6

Additional copies of this Teacher's Manual may be purchased from IEW.com/FIX-L2-T

Institute for Excellence in Writing (IEW®)
8799 N. 387 Road
Locust Grove, OK 74352
800.856.5815
info@IEW.com
IEW.com

Printed in Utah, United States of America

Accessing Your Downloads

The purchase of this book entitles its owner to a free download of the following:

- *Mastery Learning, Ability Development, and Individualized Education* e-audio
- *But, but, but ... What about Grammar?* e-audio
- *Fix It! Grammar: Town Mouse and Country Mouse* vocabulary list with definitions
- *Fix It! Grammar Glossary*

To download these e-resources, please follow the directions below:

1. Go to our website: IEW.com
2. Log in to your online customer account. If you do not have an account, you will need to create one.
3. After you are logged in, go to this web page: IEW.com/FIX-E
4. Click the red arrow, and then click the checkboxes next to the names of the files you wish to place in your account.
5. Click the "Add to my files" button.
6. To access your files now and in the future, click on "Your Account" and click on the "Files" tab (one of the gray tabs).
7. Click on each file name to download the files onto your computer.

If you have any difficulty receiving these downloads after going through the steps above, please call 800.856.5815.

Institute for Excellence in Writing
8799 N. 387 Road
Locust Grove, OK 74352

Instructions

The list below shows the components to each *Fix It! Grammar* weekly exercise.

Although **Mark It** is listed before **Fix It**, the student may choose to **Fix It** first and then **Mark It**. This is acceptable because the *Fix It! Grammar* exercises are like a word puzzle. The goal is to complete the lists at the top of the student page for each passage.

Students should discuss their work with the teacher after working through each daily passage. However, older students may work with their teacher on a weekly basis. Students should actively be involved in comparing their work with the Teacher's Manual. The repetition of finding and fixing their own mistakes allows them to recognize and avoid those mistakes in the future.

Fix It! Grammar should be treated as a game. Keep it fun!

Learn It! On the first day of the new Week, read through the Learn It section. Each Learn It covers a concept that the student will practice in future passages. Instructions for marking and fixing passages are included in each Learn It.

Read It! Read the day's passage.

Look up the bolded vocabulary word in a dictionary and pick the definition that fits the context of the story. Maintain a list of vocabulary words and their definitions.

The vocabulary definitions are printed in the Teacher's Manual.

Mark It! Mark the passage using the guide at the top of the daily practice page.

Fix It! Correct the passage using the guide at the top of the daily practice page.

The Teacher's Manual includes detailed explanations for grammar concepts and punctuation in each daily passage.

Rewrite It! After marking, correcting, and discussing the passage with the teacher, copy the corrected passage on the lines provided or into a separate notebook.

- Copy the corrected story, not the editing marks.
- Indent and use capital letters properly.
- Copy the corrected punctuation.

Appendix I Complete Story Familiarize yourself with the story that you will be editing by reading the complete story found in Appendix I.

Appendix II Collection Pages Look for strong verbs, quality adjectives, and -ly adverbs in this book and write them on the collection pages in Appendix II.

Appendix III Grammar Glossary Reference the Grammar Glossary found in Appendix III of the Teacher's Manual for more information about the concepts taught in the *Fix It! Grammar* series.

Editing Marks

¶ indent

∧ insert

delete

capitalize

lowercase

reverse order

add a space

close the space

Helpful Hints

Use different colors for **Mark It** and **Fix It**.

Additional Resource

Fix It! Grammar Cards are an optional product that will enhance the *Fix It! Grammar* learning experience.

Fix It! Grammar Cards

Thirty full color grammar cards highlight key *Fix It! Grammar* concepts for quick and easy reference.

For a more relaxed and entertaining way to drill and review grammar concepts learned, instructions for a download of multiple game ideas are included in the card pack.

Fix It! Grammar Cards are beautifully designed and come in a sturdy card box for easy storage.

IEW.com/FIX-GC

On the chart below *Fix It! Grammar Cards* are listed in the order that the information is taught in this book. Some cards are not introduced until future books.

WEEK	**Fix It! Grammar Cards for *Town Mouse and Country Mouse* Level 2**
1	Editing Marks, Capitalization, Title, Indentation, Noun
2	Pronoun
3	Preposition
4	Subject-Verb Pair, Verb, Linking Verb, Helping Verb
5	Conjunction, Coordinating Conjunction, Dependent Clause
6	Adjective
7	Interjection, Quotation
8	Number Words and Numerals
9	Adverb
10	Apostrophes
13	www Word
17	Sentence Openers
18	Prepositional Phrase
20	#3 -ly Adverb Opener
Not Used	Run-On, Clause, Indefinite Pronoun, #4 –ing Opener, Commas with Adjectives before a Noun, Comparative and Superlative Adjectives and Adverbs

Scope and Sequence

Week numbers indicate when a concept is introduced or specifically reinforced in a lesson. Once introduced the concept is practiced throughout the book.

Parts of Speech

Week	1	2	3	4	5	6	7	8	9	10	11	12	13	14	15	16	17	18	19	20	21	22	23	24	25	26	27	28	29	30
Noun	1																													
subject noun				4																										
noun of direct address												12																		
plural noun																16														
Pronoun		2																												
subject pronoun				4																										
Preposition			3								11				15			18											29	
Verb																														
action verb				4															19											
linking verb				4					9										19											
helping verb				4															19											
Coordinating Conjunction					5																		23							
Adjective						6			9																			28		
article adj	1																													
possessive adj						6										16														
adj after linking verb									9																					
Interjection							7																							
Adverb									9			12								20								28		

Capitalization

Week	1	2	3	4	5	6	7	8	9	10	11	12	13	14	15	16	17	18	19	20	21	22	23	24	25	26	27	28	29	30
First Word of Sentence	1																													
Proper Noun	1																													
Personal Pronoun I		2																												
Calendar			3																											
Interjection							7																							
Quotation Marks							7																							
Proper Adjective									9																					

Punctuation

Week	1	2	3	4	5	6	7	8	9	10	11	12	13	14	15	16	17	18	19	20	21	22	23	24	25	26	27	28	29	30
End Marks																														
period	1																													
question mark		2																												
exclamation mark			3																											
quotation marks							7																							
Commas																														
a and b					5	6																								

Week	1	2	3	4	5	6	7	8	9	10	11	12	13	14	15	16	17	18	19	20	21	22	23	24	25	26	27	28	29	30

Commas, cont.

	1	2	3	4	5	6	7	8	9	10	11	12	13	14	15	16	17	18	19	20	21	22	23	24	25	26	27	28	29	30
a, b, and c					5	6		8																						
who/which clause					5																									
that clause										10																				
noun of direct address												12																		
adverb clause													13																	
#2 prepositional opener																		18												
#3 -ly adverb opener																				20										
Quotation Marks							7					12												24						
Apostrophes																														
contraction										10																	27			
possessive adj																16														

Clauses

	1	2	3	4	5	6	7	8	9	10	11	12	13	14	15	16	17	18	19	20	21	22	23	24	25	26	27	28	29	30
Who/Which Clause					5									14																
That Clause										10				14																
Adverb Clause													13	14	15											26				

Homophones

	1	2	3	4	5	6	7	8	9	10	11	12	13	14	15	16	17	18	19	20	21	22	23	24	25	26	27	28	29	30
To/Two/Too						6																								
Its/It's							7																							
Your/You're												12																		
There/Their/They're													13																	

Other Concepts

	1	2	3	4	5	6	7	8	9	10	11	12	13	14	15	16	17	18	19	20	21	22	23	24	25	26	27	28	29	30
Indentation	1																													
Numbers								8																						
Subject-Verb Pairs				4																										

Stylistic Techniques

	1	2	3	4	5	6	7	8	9	10	11	12	13	14	15	16	17	18	19	20	21	22	23	24	25	26	27	28	29	30
Strong Verb				4																		22								
Who/Which Clause					5									14																
Quality Adjective						6																22								
-ly Adverb									9			12										22								
Adverb Clause													13	14	15															
#1 Subject Opener																	17				21									
#2 Prepositional Opener																		18			21				25					
#3 -ly Adverb Opener																				20	21				25					

Vocabulary

1 assorted overflowed adventure wicker	2 master orchard produce certain	3 snuck drowsy stifled approached	4 crept abruptly jolted tumbled	5 located eager trembled rumbled	6 noisily terrified prized dismayed
7 sturdy fetch naturally fled	8 shattered newcomer recalled lengthy	9 rumple invited elegant unfamiliar	10 recognized jittery hastily scurried	11 gasped discovered shrilly calmly	12 nervous suggested comfortable reluctantly
13 prodded ghastly offered boasted	14 digest disturbed pestered wandered	15 signaled longed confessed remarked	16 explained considered burrow wriggly	17 rarely troublesome avoided disappointed	18 apologized miserable advised cried
19 sympathetically patiently glorious refreshing	20 transported pleasant spot brilliant	21 dazzling fragrant nearly lazily	22 strolled odd exclaimed consume	23 complained ducked unusual monstrous	24 casually perfectly peculiar suspiciously
25 prompted journey declared unfortunately	26 horrendous plopped raced stuffing	27 busily collected imagined slumber	28 enormous privately savory incredibly	29 arranged intended risky protested	30 boldly provide suits prefer

Contents

Daily for an older student

Weekly Lessons

Appendices

Learn It!

Every word belongs to a word group—a part of speech. There are eight parts of speech. The first part of speech that you will learn is the noun.

8 parts of speech

For more information about nouns, see page G-5.

Noun

A **noun** names a person, place, thing, or idea.

To determine if a word is a noun, test it:

Can an article adjective (a, an, the) come before it?
Is it countable?

Noun Tests:

the ________

two ________

Find It! Read the sentence and look for the words that name people, places, things, and ideas.

Mark It! Write ***n*** above each noun as shown below.

n *n* *n*
Timmy hid behind vegetables in the garden.

A noun does not always have an article adjective before it. However, if there is an article adjective, a noun will follow it.

Article Adjective

The **article adjectives** are *a, an, the.*

A noun follows an article adjective. Sometimes adjectives (describing words) come between the article and its noun, as in *the busy mouse.*

For more information about article adjectives, see page G-14.

Mark It! Write ***ar*** above each article.

ar *ar* *ar*
A gray mouse hid behind an eggplant in the garden.

Ask students to identify the noun that follows each article.

mouse

eggplant

garden

Capitalization

Capitalize the first word of a sentence.

Capitalize proper nouns.

The word *girl* is a common noun, but *Jenny* is a proper noun.
The word *country* is a common noun, but *England* is a proper noun.

Fix It! Place three short lines below letters that should be capitalized.

the country mouse named timmy lived in england.

End Mark

Use a period at the end of a statement.

Fix It! Place a period at the end of each sentence.

Timmy loved his home.

For more information about indentation, see page G-31.

In fiction (stories), there are four reasons to start a new paragraph:

new speaker,
new topic,
new place,
new time.

Indentation

Notice that some sentences are indented. An indented sentence means that the sentence begins a new paragraph.

Read It!	Mark It!	Fix It!
johnny, the town mouse, was born in a kitchen cupboard filled with **assorted** tins of spices	2 articles (ar) 5 nouns (n)	1 capital 1 end mark

assorted
various sizes, shapes, and kinds

n johnny, *ar* the town *n* mouse, was born in *ar* a kitchen *n* cupboard filled with **assorted** *n* tins of *n* spices**.**

Capitalization	***Johnny*** proper noun; first word of the sentence
End Marks	Use a period at the end of a statement.
Note	In this sentence *town* and *kitchen* are not nouns. They are adjectives.

Rewrite It! Johnny, the town mouse, was born in a kitchen cupboard filled with assorted tins of spices.

Read It!	Mark It!	Fix It!
timmy, the country mouse, was born in a garden. it **overflowed** with vegetables	2 articles (ar) 4 nouns (n)	2 capitals 1 end mark

overflowed
filled with a huge quantity

n timmy, *ar* the country *n* mouse, was born in *ar* a *n* garden.

it **overflowed** with *n* vegetables.

Capitalization	***Timmy*** proper noun; first word of the sentence ***It*** first word of the sentence
End Marks	Use a period at the end of a statement.
Note	In this sentence *country* is not a noun. It is an adjective.

Rewrite It! Timmy, the country mouse, was born in a garden. It overflowed with vegetables.

Read It!	Mark It!	Fix It!
the two mice lived a long way from each other. an **adventure** brought them together	3 articles (ar) 3 nouns (n)	2 capitals 1 end mark

adventure
exciting experience

ar n ar n
the two mice lived a long way from each other.

ar n
an **adventure** brought them together.

Capitalization	***The***; ***An*** first word of the sentence
End Marks	Use a period at the end of a statement.

Rewrite It! The two mice lived a long way from each other. An adventure brought them together.

Read It!	Mark It!	Fix It!
it all started when timmy traveled to town by mistake in a **wicker** basket	1 article (ar) 4 nouns (n)	2 capitals 1 end mark

wicker
made of thin twigs woven together

it all started when timmy (n) traveled to town (n) by mistake (n) in a (ar) **wicker** basket (n).

Capitalization	***It*** first word of the sentence ***Timmy*** proper noun
End Marks	Use a period at the end of a statement.

Rewrite It! It all started when Timmy traveled to town by mistake in a wicker basket.

Learn It!

Pronoun

A **pronoun** replaces a noun in order to avoid repetition. It refers back to some person or thing recently mentioned and takes the place of that person or thing.

There are many types of pronouns. The personal pronouns take the place of common and proper nouns. The personal pronouns in the table below are organized by number, person, and function.

Number means one (singular) or more than one (plural).
Person means who is speaking (1st), spoken to (2nd), or spoken about (3rd).
Function means the job a word is doing in the sentence.

2 numbers	3 persons	These pronouns can function as the subject of a sentence.	These pronouns can function as the object of a preposition.	These possessive pronouns function as adjectives.	These possessive pronouns do not function as adjectives.
singular	*1st*	I	me	my	mine
	2nd	you	you	your	yours
	3rd	he, she, it	him, her, it	his, her, its	his, hers, its
plural	*1st*	we	us	our	ours
	2nd	you	you	your	yours
	3rd	they	them	their	theirs

Mark It! Write ***pr*** above each pronoun.

                                          pr
Timmy traveled to town. It was busy with many people.
pr   ***pr***   ***pr***
He was scared of them and their noise.

Without pronouns to replace the nouns, this passage sounds strange.

Timmy traveled to town. The town was busy with many people.
Timmy was scared of the people and the people's noise.

For more information about pronouns, see page G-6.

The noun the pronoun replaces is called the antecedent.

Ask students to identify the nouns that the pronouns replace.

It replaces *town*
He replaces *Timmy*
them replaces *people*
their replaces *people's*

Week 6 students will learn a possessive pronoun like *their* replaces a possessive noun like *people's*. Both function as adjectives.

Capitalization

Capitalize the personal pronoun *I*.

Fix It! Place three short lines below the personal pronoun *I*.

When the basket opened, i jumped out.

End Mark

Use a question mark at the end of a question.

Fix It! Place a question mark at the end of each question.

Did Johnny live in a fancy house**?**

Read It!	Mark It!	Fix It!
the basket belonged to a **master** gardener, who lived in northern england. what did he grow	2 articles (ar) 3 nouns (n) 1 pronoun (pr)	3 capitals 1 end mark

master
skilled; experienced

the basket belonged to a **master** gardener,

who lived in northern england. what did he grow**?**

Capitalization	***The***; ***What*** first word of the sentence ***England*** proper noun
End Marks	Use a question mark at the end of a question.
Pronoun	***he*** replaces *master gardener*
Note	In this sentence *master* is not a noun. It is an adjective.

Rewrite It! The basket belonged to a master gardener, who lived in northern England. What did he grow?

Read It!	Mark It!	Fix It!
he grew vegetables in his garden and fruit in his **orchard**	4 nouns (n) 3 pronouns (pr)	1 capital 1 end mark

orchard
land devoted to growing fruit or nut trees

pr n pr n n
he grew vegetables in his garden and fruit

pr n
in his **orchard.**

Capitalization	***He*** first word of the sentence
End Marks	Use a period at the end of a statement.
Pronoun	***He*** replaces master gardener ***his***; ***his*** replace master gardener's Week 6 students will learn that a possessive pronoun like *his* is a pronoun that functions as an adjective.

Rewrite It! He grew vegetables in his garden and fruit in his orchard.

Read It!	Mark It!	Fix It!
each week he filled a basket with fresh **produce**. then he set it by the gate	2 articles (ar) 4 nouns (n) 3 pronouns (pr)	2 capitals 1 end mark

produce
vegetables and fruits that are grown or produced to be sold

each (n) week (pr) he filled (ar) a (n) basket with fresh (n) **produce**.

then (pr) he set (pr) it by (ar) the (n) gate.

Capitalization	***Each***; ***Then*** first word of the sentence
End Marks	Use a period at the end of a statement.
Pronoun	***he***; ***he*** replace *master gardener* ***it*** replaces *basket*

Rewrite It! Each week he filled a basket with fresh produce. Then he set it by the gate.

Read It!	Mark It!	Fix It!
on **certain** days a carrier came. he took the wicker basket to town on a cart	3 articles (ar) 5 nouns (n) 1 pronoun (pr)	2 capitals 1 end mark

certain
agreed upon; fixed

on **certain** days a carrier came. he took the wicker basket to town on a cart.

Capitalization	***On***; ***He*** first word of the sentence
End Marks	Use a period at the end of a statement.
Pronoun	***He*** replaces *carrier*

Rewrite It! On certain days a carrier came. He took the wicker basket to town on a cart.

Learn It!

Preposition

A **preposition** starts a phrase that shows the relationship between a noun or pronoun and another word in the sentence.

A prepositional phrase always begins with a preposition and ends with a noun or pronoun. The phrase may have adjectives in between but never a verb.

The noun or pronoun that ends the prepositional phrase is called the object of the preposition. When the object of the preposition is a pronoun, it will be one of the objective case pronouns: *me, you, him, her, it, us, you, them.*

Memorize It! **preposition + noun (no verb)**

Find It! Use the list below to find the prepositions in the sentence.

Once you find a preposition, ask "What?" to identify the noun or pronoun that ends the prepositional phrase.

Mark It! Underline each prepositional phrase. Start the line under the preposition and end with the noun.

Near the garden Timmy climbed into a large basket that was filled with vegetables.

Prepositions List

aboard	around	between	in	opposite	toward
about	as	beyond	inside	out	under
above	at	by	instead of	outside	underneath
according to	because of	concerning	into	over	unlike
across	before	despite	like	past	until
after	behind	down	minus	regarding	unto
against	below	during	near	since	up, upon
along	beneath	except	of	through	with
amid	beside	for	off	throughout	within
among	besides	from	on, onto	to	without

For more information about prepositions, see page G-8.

Ask students to identify the prepositional phrase and explain how it follows the pattern.

near what? ***garden***
Near the garden starts with a preposition (near) and ends with a noun (garden). It has an article in between but no verb.

into what? ***basket***
into a large basket starts with a preposition (into) and ends with a noun (basket). It has an article and an adjective in between but no verb.

with what? ***vegetables***
with vegetables starts with a preposition (with) and ends with a noun (vegetables).

When *to* is followed by a verb, as in *to finish*, it is called an infinitive. It does not fit the prepositional phrase pattern because *finish* is not a noun or pronoun. Do not mark infinitives as prepositional phrases.

Capitalization

Capitalize days of the week and months of the year.

Do not capitalize seasons: spring, summer, fall, winter.

Fix It! Place three short lines below letters that should be capitalized.

On a wednesday that summer in june, Timmy ate peas.

End Mark

Use an exclamation mark at the end of a sentence that expresses strong emotion.

Fix It! Place an exclamation mark at the end of each exclamatory sentence.

Timmy was starving**!**

Read It! | **Mark It!** | **Fix It!**

early one monday in april, timmy **snuck** into the garden. the peas looked delicious

2 articles (ar)
5 nouns (n)
2 prepositional phrases

5 capitals
1 end mark

snuck
moved quietly and secretly

early one monday in april, timmy **snuck** into the garden. the peas looked delicious**!**

Capitalization	***Early***; ***The*** first word of the sentence ***Monday***; ***April***; ***Timmy*** proper noun
End Marks	Use an exclamation mark at the end of a sentence that expresses strong emotion.

Rewrite It! Early one Monday in April, Timmy snuck into the garden. The peas looked delicious!

Read It!	Mark It!	Fix It!
there he sat with his mouth stuffed full of spring peas. the large meal made him **drowsy**	1 article (ar) 3 nouns (n) 3 pronouns (pr) 2 prepositional phrases	2 capitals 1 end mark

drowsy
sleepy

pr *pr* *n* *n*
there he sat with his mouth stuffed full of spring peas.

ar *n* *pr*
the large meal made him **drowsy.**

Capitalization	***There***; ***The*** first word of the sentence
End Marks	Use a period at the end of a statement.
Pronoun	***he***; ***him*** replace *Timmy* ***his*** replaces *Timmy's*
Note	Week 6 students will learn that a possessive pronoun like *his* is a pronoun that functions as an adjective. In this sentence *spring* is not a noun. It is an adjective.

Rewrite It! There he sat with his mouth stuffed full of spring peas. The large meal made him drowsy.

Read It!	Mark It!	Fix It!
timmy stretched his paws and **stifled** a yawn. where could he take a nap	2 articles (ar) 4 nouns (n) 2 pronouns (pr)	2 capitals 1 end mark

stifled
withheld; kept from making

timmy (n) stretched his (pr) paws (n) and **stifled** a (ar) yawn (n).

where could he (pr) take a (ar) nap (n)**?**

Capitalization	***Timmy*** proper noun; first word of the sentence ***Where*** first word of the sentence
End Marks	Use a question mark at the end of a question.
Pronoun	***his*** replaces *Timmy's* ***he*** replaces *Timmy*
Note	Week 6 students will learn that a possessive pronoun like *his* is a pronoun that functions as an adjective.

Rewrite It! Timmy stretched his paws and stifled a yawn. Where could he take a nap?

Read It!	**Mark It!**	**Fix It!**
timmy noticed a basket beside the gate. he **approached** it without a sound	3 articles (ar) 4 nouns (n) 2 pronouns (pr) 2 prepositional phrases	2 capitals 1 end mark

approached
came near

timmy (n) noticed a (ar) basket (n) beside the (ar) gate (n). he (pr) **approached** it (pr) without a (ar) sound (n).

Capitalization	***Timmy*** proper noun; first word of the sentence ***He*** first word of the sentence
End Marks	Use a period at the end of a statement.
Pronoun	***He*** replaces *Timmy* ***it*** replaces *basket*

Rewrite It! Timmy noticed a basket beside the gate. He approached it without a sound.

Learn It!

Verb

A **verb** shows action, links the subject to another word, or helps another verb. To determine if a word is a verb, use the verb test.

An **action verb** shows action or ownership.

A **linking verb** links the subject to a noun or adjective. The words below are linking verbs.

Memorize It! **am, is, are, was, were, be, being, been**
seem, become, appear, grow, remain
taste, sound, smell, feel, look

A **helping verb** helps an action verb or a linking verb. The helping verb is always followed by another verb. The words below are helping verbs.

Memorize It! **am, is, are, was, were, be, being, been**
have, has, had, do, does, did, may, might, must
can, will, shall, could, would, should

Every verb has a subject. The subject and verb (s v) belong together.

Subject

A **subject** is a noun or pronoun that performs a verb action. It tells who or what the clause is about.

To find a subject, ask who or what is doing the verb.

Only nouns and pronouns can function as subjects. When the subject is a pronoun, it will be one of the subjective case pronouns: *I, you, he, she, it, we, you, they, who,* or *which.*

Find It! Read the sentence and look for the verb.
Ask, "Who or what ___ (verb)?"

Mark It! Write *v* above each verb and *s* above each subject.

Timmy (s) climbed (v) into the basket. He (s) was (v) a young mouse.

Timmy (s) had (v) decided (v) to take a nap.

For more information about verbs, see page G-9.

Verb Test:

I ___.

It ___.

Some verbs function as either action or linking verbs.

He *felt* (action) the basket's edge.

He *felt* (linking) tired.

If you can substitute *is* for the verb, it is probably functioning as a linking verb.

For more information about subjects and s v pairs, see pages G-7, G-17.

Ask students to identify the subjects and verbs.

What is the verb? ***climbed***

Who climbed? ***Timmy***

What is the verb? ***was***

Who was? ***He***

What is the verb? ***had decided***

Who had decided? ***Timmy***

When *to* is followed by a verb, as in *to take*, it is called an infinitive. It does not function as a verb because *to take* does not have a subject. Do not mark infinitives as verbs.

Because a word that ends in -ing rarely functions as a verb, do not allow students to list -ing words on the Strong Verb collection page.

Strong Verb

A **strong verb** dresses up writing because it creates a strong image or feeling. A strong verb is an action verb, never a linking or helping verb. Look for strong verbs in this book and write them on the Strong Verb collection page, Appendix II.

Think About It!

According to the verb definition, there are three categories of verbs: action, linking, helping. Every clause has an action verb or a linking verb. When a helping verb helps either an action verb or a linking verb, the two verbs together are called the verb phrase.

Action: Timmy climbed into the basket.

In this sentence *climbed* is the action verb. *Climbed* is the action that Timmy is doing.

Linking: Timmy felt sleepy.

In this sentence *felt* is the linking verb. *Felt* links the subject *Timmy* to the adjective *sleepy*.

Helping + Action: Timmy had climbed into the basket.

In this sentence *had* is a helping verb helping the action verb *climbed*. *Had climbed* is the verb phrase.

Helping + Linking: Timmy did feel sleepy.

In this sentence *did* is a helping verb helping the linking verb *feel*. *Did feel* is the verb phrase.

The first eight words are called *be* verbs. They appear on both the Linking Verbs and Helping Verbs Lists.

Linking Verbs List

am, is, are, was, were, be, being, been (*be* verbs)

seem, become, appear, grow, remain

taste, sound, smell, feel, look (verbs dealing with the senses)

Helping Verbs List

am, is, are, was, were, be, being, been (*be* verbs)

have, has, had, do, does, did, may, might, must

can, will, shall, could, would, should

Read It!	Mark It!	Fix It!
he **crept** into the basket and was soon asleep. it was perfect **crept** moved slowly and close to the ground	1 article (ar) 1 noun (n) 2 pronouns (pr) 1 prepositional phrase 2 subject-verb pairs (s v)	2 capitals 1 end mark

s pr: he; v: **crept**; into the basket (prepositional phrase; ar: the; n: basket); v: was

he **crept** into the basket and was soon asleep.

s pr: it; v: was

it was perfect**!**

Capitalization	***He***; ***It*** first word of the sentence
End Marks	Use an exclamation mark at the end of a sentence that expresses strong emotion.
Pronoun	***He*** replaces *Timmy* ***It*** replaces *basket*
S V Pairs	***He crept***, ***was***; ***It was***

Rewrite It! He crept into the basket and was soon asleep. It was perfect!

Read It!

timmy awoke **abruptly** in a fright, and the basket was lifted onto a cart

Mark It!

3 articles (ar)
4 nouns (n)
2 prepositional phrases
2 subject-verb pairs (s v)

Fix It!

1 capital
1 end mark

abruptly
suddenly and unexpectedly

timmy (s, n) awoke (v) **abruptly** in a (ar) fright (n), and the (ar) basket (s, n) was (v) lifted (v) onto a (ar) cart (n).

Capitalization	***Timmy*** proper noun; first word of the sentence
End Marks	Use a period at the end of a statement.
S V Pairs	***Timmy awoke***; ***basket was lifted***

Rewrite It! Timmy awoke abruptly in a fright, and the basket was lifted onto a cart.

Read It!	Mark It!	Fix It!
suddenly the cart **jolted**, and the horse trotted to town	2 articles (ar) 3 nouns (n) 1 prepositional phrase 2 subject-verb pairs (s v)	1 capital 1 end mark

jolted
shook roughly

suddenly the cart **jolted**, and the horse trotted to town.

Capitalization	***Suddenly*** first word of the sentence
End Marks	Use a period at the end of a statement.
S V Pairs	***cart jolted***; ***horse trotted***

Rewrite It! Suddenly the cart jolted, and the horse trotted to town.

Read It!	Mark It!	Fix It!
for two miles timmy was **tumbled** around inside the basket	1 article (ar) 3 nouns (n) 2 prepositional phrases 1 subject-verb pair (s v)	2 capitals 1 end mark

tumbled
rolled around; tossed about

for two miles timmy was **tumbled** around inside the basket.

Capitalization	***For*** first word of the sentence ***Timmy*** proper noun
End Marks	Use a period at the end of a statement.
S V Pairs	***Timmy was tumbled***
Note	In this sentence *around* is an adverb. It is not a preposition because it is not followed by a noun. **PATTERN preposition + noun (no verb)**

Rewrite It! For two miles Timmy was tumbled around inside the basket.

Learn It!

Conjunction

A conjunction connects words, phrases, or clauses.

A **coordinating conjunction** connects the same type of words, phrases, or clauses.

The items the coordinating conjunction connects must be grammatically the same: two or more nouns, two or more verbs, two or more prepositional phrases, and so forth.

Timmy ran to the basket and opened it.

The coordinating conjunction *and* connects *ran* (verb) and *opened* (verb) because these words are grammatically the same type of words (verbs).

The coordinating conjunction *and* does not connect *basket* (noun) and *opened* (verb) because a noun and a verb are not grammatically the same type of words.

Use the acronym FANBOYS to learn the seven coordinating conjunctions.

Memorize It!

F	A	N	B	O	Y	S
for	and	nor	but	or	yet	so

Mark It! Write *cc* above each coordinating conjunction.

The carrier delivered the basket, tipped his hat, *cc* and left.

The cook saw the vegetables *cc* but not the mouse.

Comma

A **comma** is used to separate items in a sentence. This week you will learn two comma rules. Copy the commas correctly when you rewrite the passages.

Do not use a comma before a coordinating conjunction when it connects two items in a series unless they are main clauses.
PATTERN a and b

Use commas to separate three or more items in a series.
PATTERN a, b, and c

For more information about coordinating conjunctions, see page G-12.

An acronym is a word formed from the first letters of other words.

Ask students to identify the coordinating conjunction and explain what it connects.

And connects three verbs: *delivered, tipped, left.* Use commas.
a, b, and c

But connects two nouns: *vegetables, mouse.* Do not use a comma. a and b

Draw students' attention to the comma patterns.

Require students to copy the commas correctly when they rewrite the passages.

For more information about *who/which* clauses, see page G-39.

When *who* or *which* begins a *who/which* clause, it is a relative pronoun.

Students will not mark *who* or *which* as a pronoun but will mark it with w/w.

When *who* or *which* begins a sentence, it asks a question. It is not a *who/which* clause dress-up.

Ask students to identify the subject and verb in the *who/which* clause and to identify the noun that the clause describes.

What is the verb? ***crept***

Who crept? ***who***
The relative pronoun *who* replaces the noun *Timmy*.

who crept into the basket describes *Timmy*

What is the verb? ***took***

Who took? ***carrier***
The relative pronoun *which* replaces the noun *basket*.

which the carrier took to town describes *basket*

The complete comma rule is to place commas around a *who/which* clause unless it is essential to the meaning of the sentence. At this level, students do not need to determine if a clause is essential or nonessential.

Who/Which Clause

A ***who/which* clause** is a group of words that describes the noun it follows.

A *who/which* clause begins with the word *who* or *which,* a type of pronoun.

Who refers to people, personified animals, and pets.
Which refers to things, animals, and places.

A *who/which* clause must be added to a sentence that is already complete.

The cook saw the mouse. ***(sentence)***

The cook, who saw the mouse. ***(fragment)***

The cook, who saw the mouse, screamed. ***(sentence)***

The cook, who screamed, saw the mouse. ***(sentence)***

A *who/which* clause contains a subject and a verb. The subject of most *who/which* clauses is *who* or *which,* but sometimes the subject is another word in the clause.

Mark It! Place parentheses around the *who/which* clause and write **w/w** above the word *who* or *which*. Write **v** above each verb and **s** above each subject.

s **v**
w/w
Timmy, **(**who crept into the basket**)**, was soon asleep.

s **v**
w/w
Timmy slept in the basket, **(**which the carrier took to town**)**.

, Place commas around a *who/which* clause.

Read It!	Mark It!	Fix It!
finally, the horse and cart stopped at a fancy house, which was **located** in a large town	3 articles (ar) 4 nouns (n) 1 coordinating conjunction (cc) 2 prepositional phrases 1 *who/which* clause (w/w) 2 subject-verb pairs (s v)	1 capital 1 end mark

located
set or settled in a certain place

ar (the), s n (horse), cc (and), s n (cart), v (stopped), ar (a)

finally, the horse and cart stopped at a

n (house), w/w (which), s, v (was), v (located), ar (a), n (town)

fancy house, (which was **located** in a large town).

Capitalization	***Finally*** first word of the sentence
End Marks	Use a period at the end of a statement.
W/W Clause	***which was located in a large town*** describes *house*
S V Pairs	***horse**, **cart stopped**; **which was located***

Rewrite It! Finally, the horse and cart stopped at a fancy house, which was located in a large town.

Read It!	Mark It!	Fix It!
the carrier, who was **eager** to finish his job, set the basket in the kitchen	3 articles (ar) 4 nouns (n) 1 pronoun (pr) 1 prepositional phrase 1 *who/which* clause (w/w) 2 subject-verb pairs (s v)	1 capital 1 end mark

eager
having great desire

the carrier, (who was **eager** to finish his job),
set the basket in the kitchen.

Capitalization	***The*** first word of the sentence
End Marks	Use a period at the end of a statement.
Pronoun	***his*** replaces *carrier's*
W/W Clause	***who was eager to finish his job*** describes *carrier*
S V Pairs	***carrier set***; ***who was***
Note	The phrase *to finish* does not follow the **PATTERN preposition + noun (no verb)**. When *to* is followed by a verb, it is called an infinitive. Do not mark infinitives as prepositional phrases because they include a verb. Do not mark infinitives as verbs because they do not have a subject. They function as neither a prepositional phrase nor a verb.

Rewrite It! The carrier, who was eager to finish his job, set the basket in the kitchen.

Read It!	Mark It!	Fix It!
timmy heard the slam of the backdoor. he **trembled** with fear but was unharmed	2 articles (ar) 4 nouns (n) 1 pronoun (pr) 1 coordinating conjunction (cc) 2 prepositional phrases 2 subject-verb pairs (s v)	2 capitals 1 end mark

trembled
shook involuntarily

timmy heard the slam of the backdoor.
he **trembled** with fear but was unharmed.

Capitalization	***Timmy*** proper noun; first word of the sentence ***He*** first word of the sentence
End Marks	Use a period at the end of a statement.
Pronoun	***He*** replaces *Timmy*
S V Pairs	***Timmy heard***; ***He trembled***, ***was***

Rewrite It! Timmy heard the slam of the backdoor. He trembled with fear but was unharmed.

Read It!	Mark It!	Fix It!
shortly after, the horse and cart **rumbled** away	1 article (ar) 2 nouns (n) 1 coordinating conjunction (cc) 1 subject-verb pair (s v)	1 capital 1 end mark

rumbled
moved with a deep, heavy sound like thunder

s̲hortly after, the*ar* horse*s n* and*cc* cart*s n* **rumbled***v* away.

Capitalization	***Shortly*** first word of the sentence
End Marks	Use a period at the end of a statement.
S V Pairs	***horse***, ***cart rumbled***
Note	In this sentence *after* is not a preposition because it is not followed by a noun. **PATTERN preposition + noun (no verb).**

Rewrite It! Shortly after, the horse and cart rumbled away.

Learn It!

Adjective

An **adjective** describes a noun or pronoun.

An adjective tells which one, what kind, how many, or whose.

Memorize It! **which one? what kind? how many? whose?**

An article adjective (a, an, the) is a special type of adjective that signals that a noun is coming. You can test if a word is an adjective by putting the word between an article and a noun.

The scared mice ran.

An adjective usually comes before the word it describes.
The adjective *scared* describes *mice*. What kind of mice? *scared*

The mouse ran to his nest.

Because the possessive pronouns *my, your, his, her, its, our, their* function as adjectives, you will now mark them as adjectives.
The pronoun *his* replaces *mouse's* and functions as an adjective.
Whose nest? *his*

Find It! Find the nouns and pronouns in the sentence.

Once you find a noun or pronoun, ask the adjective questions to identify the adjectives.

Mark It! Write ***adj*** above each adjective.

adj ***adj*** ***adj***
Two scared mice jumped from the first basket and ran
adj ***adj***
under the cook's nose. Their hearts raced with fear.

Quality Adjective

A **quality adjective** dresses up writing because it creates a strong image or feeling. A quality adjective is more specific than a weak adjective. A weak adjective is overused, boring, or vague. Look for quality adjectives in this book and write them on the Quality Adjective collection page, Appendix II.

For more information about adjectives, see page G-14.

Adjective Test:

the ____ pen

Students will continue to write ***ar*** above article adjectives.

Ask students to find nouns (or pronouns) and then ask questions to identify adjectives.

What kind of mice? ***scared***

How many scared mice? ***two***

Which basket? ***first***

Whose nose? ***cook's***

Whose hearts? ***their***

A possessive noun like *cook's* is a noun functioning as an adjective in order to show ownership.

A possessive pronoun like *their* is a pronoun functioning as an adjective in order to show ownership.

For more information about homophones, see page G-35.

Homophone

A **homophone** is a word that sounds like another word but is spelled differently and has a different meaning. Correctly use the homophones *to, two,* and *too.*

To is a preposition or part of an infinitive: *to town* (preposition); *to hide* (infinitive).

Two is a number: *two mice* (2 mice).

Too is an adverb meaning also or to an excessive degree: *had it too; too long.*

Fix It! Place a line through the incorrect homophone and write the correct word above it.

Mark It! If the correct homophone is an adjective, write ***adj*** above the corrected word. If it is a preposition, underline the prepositional phrase.

The ~~to~~ *two* (adj) mice lived ~~to~~ *too* far from each other ~~too~~ *to* meet.

They did not travel <u>~~too~~ *to* town</u> together.

Comma

A **comma** is used to separate items in a sentence. Week 5 you learned two comma rules to use with coordinating conjunctions: a and b; a, b, and c. This week you will correct errors with *a* and *b.*

Ask students to identify the coordinating conjunction and explain what it connects. If it connects two items that are not main clauses, do not use a comma.

And connects two verbs: *saw, screamed.* Do not use a comma. a and b

Find It! Find the coordinating conjunction. Count how many items it connects.

Fix It! If there is a comma before a coordinating conjunction that connects only two items, remove it.

The cook saw (v) Timmy, and (cc) screamed (v)**!**

Read It!	Mark It!	Fix It!
inside the large house sarah, the maid, **noisily** raced up the stairs and down the stairs to	4 articles (ar) 5 nouns (n) 1 adjective (adj) 1 coordinating conjunction (cc) 3 prepositional phrases 1 subject-verb pair (s v)	2 capitals 1 end mark 1 homophone

noisily
loudly

inside(ar) the(adj) large(n) house (s n) sarah, (ar) the (n) maid, **noisily** (v) raced up (ar) the (n) stairs (cc) and down (ar) the (n) stairs ~~to~~ (too).

Capitalization	***Inside*** first word of the sentence ***Sarah*** proper noun
End Marks	Use a period at the end of a statement.
Adjective	What kind of house? ***large***
S V Pairs	***Sarah raced***
Homophones	Use ***too***, which means also in this sentence.

Rewrite It! Inside the large house Sarah, the maid, noisily raced up the stairs and down the stairs too.

Read It!	Mark It!	Fix It!
the many noises **terrified** timmy. he had lived his entire life in the peaceful, and quiet country	2 articles (ar) 4 nouns (n) 1 pronoun (pr) 5 adjectives (adj) 1 coordinating conjunction (cc) 1 prepositional phrase 2 subject-verb pairs (s v)	3 capitals 1 comma 1 end mark

terrified
made very afraid

the many noises **terrified** timmy. he had lived
his entire life in the peaceful, and quiet country.

Capitalization	***The***; ***He*** first word of the sentence ***Timmy*** proper noun
End Marks	Use a period at the end of a statement.
Pronoun	***He*** replaces *Timmy*
Adjective	How many noises? ***many*** How much of life? ***entire*** *How much* is a form of the adjective question *how many*. Whose entire life? ***his*** The possessive pronoun *his* functions as an adjective. What kind of country? ***peaceful*** *and* ***quiet***
S V Pairs	***noises terrified***; ***He had lived***
Commas	Do not use a comma to separate two items connected with a coordinating conjunction. **PATTERN a and b** *peaceful* and *quiet*

Rewrite It! The many noises terrified Timmy. He had lived his entire life in the peaceful and quiet country.

Read It!	Mark It!	Fix It!
soon julia, the cook, opened, and unpacked the basket, which contained **prized** vegetables	2 articles (ar) 4 nouns (n) 1 adjective (adj) 1 coordinating conjunction (cc) 1 *who/which* clause (w/w) 2 subject-verb pairs (s v)	2 capitals 1 comma 1 end mark

prized
highly valued

soon julia, the cook, opened, and unpacked the basket, (which contained **prized** vegetables).

Capitalization	***Soon*** first word of the sentence ***Julia*** proper noun
End Marks	Use a period at the end of a statement.
Adjective	What kind of vegetables? ***prized***
W/W Clause	***which contained prized vegetables*** describes *basket*
S V Pairs	***Julia opened***, ***unpacked***; ***which contained***
Commas	Do not use a comma to separate two items connected with a coordinating conjunction. PATTERN **a and b** *opened* and *unpacked*

Rewrite It! Soon Julia, the cook, opened and unpacked the basket, which contained prized vegetables.

Read It!	Mark It!	Fix It!
suddenly timmy jumped out of the basket. the tiny mouse surprised, and **dismayed** julia	2 articles (ar) 4 nouns (n) 1 adjective (adj) 1 coordinating conjunction (cc) 1 prepositional phrase 2 subject-verb pairs (s v)	4 capitals 1 comma 1 end mark

dismayed
alarmed; surprised in a negative way

suddenly timmy jumped out of the basket.

the tiny mouse surprised, and **dismayed** julia.

Capitalization	***Suddenly***; ***The*** first word of the sentence ***Timmy***; ***Julia*** proper noun
End Marks	Use a period at the end of a statement.
Adjective	What kind of mouse? ***tiny***
S V Pairs	***Timmy jumped***; ***mouse surprised, dismayed***
Commas	Do not use a comma to separate two items connected with a coordinating conjunction. **PATTERN a and b** *surprised* and *dismayed*

Rewrite It! Suddenly Timmy jumped out of the basket. The tiny mouse surprised and dismayed Julia.

Learn It!

Interjection

An **interjection** expresses an emotion.

When an interjection expresses a strong emotion, use an exclamation mark. When an interjection does not express a strong emotion, use a comma.

Mark It! Write ***int*** above each interjection.

int
Yikes**!** The cat is coming**!**

For more information about interjections, see page G-15

Capitalization

Capitalize an interjection when it is the first word of a sentence.

Capitalize a word that follows an exclamation mark.

Fix It! Place three short lines below letters that should be capitalized.

oh! where can we hide? ah, this is good.

Homophone

A **homophone** is a word that sounds like another word but is spelled differently and has a different meaning. Correctly use the homophones *its* and *it's*.

Its is a possessive pronoun: *its handle* (the handle belongs to it).

The possessive pronoun *its* tells whose and functions as an adjective.

It's is a contraction: *it's morning* (it is morning).

The contraction *it's* is a shortened form of *it is* and functions as the subject pronoun (it) and verb (is) of the clause.

A contraction uses an apostrophe to show where a letter or letters have been removed.

Fix It! Place a line through the incorrect homophone and write the correct word above it.

Mark It! If the correct homophone is *its,* write ***adj*** above *its.*
If the correct homophone is *it's,* write ***pr*** and ***s*** above *it.*
Write ***v*** above *'s.*

s v / ***pr*** / ***It's*** — ***adj*** / ***its***
~~Its~~ too bad the cat still has ~~it's~~ claws.

For more information about quotation marks, see page G-27.

Quotation Marks—Capitalization and End Marks

Quotation marks indicate words are spoken.

Quote "I cannot find the poker," **Attribution** the maid said.

The quote is the sentence in quotation marks. The attribution is the person speaking and the speaking verb.

Capitalize the first word of a quoted sentence.

Capitalize the first word of an attribution when it begins the sentence.

Do not capitalize the first word of an attribution when it follows the quote.

Attribution, "**Q**uote." "**Q**uote," attribution.

Fix It! Place three short lines below letters that should be capitalized

julia exclaimed, "call the cat!"

If the quoted sentence makes a statement, place a period inside the closing quotation mark unless the attribution follows.

Attribution, "Quote**.**" "Quote," attribution.

If the quoted sentence asks a question, place a question mark inside the closing quotation mark.

Attribution, "Quote**?**" "Quote**?**" attribution.

If the quoted sentence expresses strong emotion, place an exclamation mark inside the closing quotation mark.

Attribution, "Quote**!**" "Quote**!**" attribution.

Fix It! Place an exclamation mark at the end of a sentence that expresses strong emotion.

Julia exclaimed, "Call the cat**!**"

Read It!	Mark It!	Fix It!
julia jumped onto a **sturdy** chair, and shouted, "eek! its a mouse **sturdy** strongly built	2 articles (ar) 3 nouns (n) 1 pronoun (pr) 1 adjective (adj) 1 coordinating conjunction (cc) 1 interjection (int) 1 prepositional phrase 2 subject-verb pairs (s v)	3 capitals 1 comma 1 end mark 1 homophone

julia jumped onto a **sturdy** chair, and shouted, "eek! its a mouse**!**

No closing quotation mark because quote continues.

Capitalization	***Julia*** proper noun; first word of the sentence ***Eek*** first word of the quoted sentence ***It's*** first word following an interjection that uses an exclamation mark
End Marks	Use an exclamation mark at the end of a sentence that expresses strong emotion.
Pronoun	***It*** replaces *mouse*
Adjective	What kind of chair? ***sturdy***
S V Pairs	***Julia jumped, shouted***; ***It's*** The contraction *It's* includes both a subject (It) and a verb (is).
Commas	Do not use a comma to separate two items connected with a coordinating conjunction. **PATTERN a and b** *jumped* and *shouted*
Homophones	Use ***It's***, the contraction for *it is*.

Rewrite It! Julia jumped onto a sturdy chair and shouted, "Eek! It's a mouse!

Read It!	Mark It!	Fix It!
aah! i need help! sarah, you **fetch** the long poker! where is the cat"	2 articles (ar) 4 nouns (n) 2 pronouns (pr) 1 adjective (adj) 1 interjection (int) 3 subject-verb pairs (s v)	4 capitals 1 end mark

fetch
go and bring back

No opening quotation mark because quote continues.

aah! i need help! sarah, you **fetch** the long poker!
where is the cat**?**"

Capitalization	***Aah*** first word of the quoted sentence ***I*** personal pronoun I; first word following an interjection that uses an exclamation mark ***Sarah*** proper noun; first word of the quoted sentence ***Where*** first word of the quoted sentence
End Marks	Use a question mark at the end of a question. Place it inside the closing quotation mark.
Pronoun	***I*** replaces *Julia* ***you*** replaces *Sarah*
Adjective	What kind of poker? ***long***
S V Pairs	***I need***; ***you fetch***; ***cat is***

Rewrite It! Aah! I need help! Sarah, you fetch the long poker! Where is the cat?"

Read It!	Mark It!	Fix It!
naturally, timmy did not wait for the long poker, or the hungry cat, who was oddly named catnap	2 articles (ar) 4 nouns (n) 2 adjectives (adj) 1 coordinating conjunction (cc) 1 prepositional phrase 1 *who/which* clause (w/w) 2 subject-verb pairs (s v)	3 capitals 1 comma 1 end mark

naturally
of course

naturally, timmy did not wait for the long poker, or the hungry cat, (who was oddly named catnap).

Capitalization	***Naturally*** first word of the sentence ***Timmy***; ***Catnap*** proper noun
End Marks	Use a period at the end of a statement.
Adjective	What kind of poker? ***long*** What kind of cat? ***hungry***
W/W Clause	***who was oddly named Catnap*** describes *cat*
S V Pairs	***Timmy did wait***; ***who was named***
Commas	Do not use a comma to separate two items connected with a coordinating conjunction. **PATTERN a and b** *poker* or *cat*

Rewrite It! Naturally, Timmy did not wait for the long poker or the hungry cat, who was oddly named Catnap.

Read It!	Mark It!	Fix It!
timmy **fled** along the baseboard, and popped into a narrow hole at it's edge	2 articles (ar)	1 capital
	4 nouns (n)	1 comma
	2 adjectives (adj)	1 end mark
	1 coordinating conjunction (cc)	1 homophone
fled ran away from danger	3 prepositional phrases	
	1 subject-verb pair (s v)	

timmy **fled** along the baseboard, and popped into a narrow hole at ~~it's~~ its edge.

Capitalization	***Timmy*** proper noun; first word of the sentence
End Marks	Use a period at the end of a statement.
Adjective	What kind of hole? ***narrow*** Whose edge? ***its*** The possessive pronoun *its* functions as an adjective.
S V Pairs	***Timmy fled, popped***
Commas	Do not use a comma to separate two items connected with a coordinating conjunction. **PATTERN a and b** *fled* and *popped*
Homophones	Use ***its***, the possessive pronoun.

Rewrite It! Timmy fled along the baseboard and popped into a narrow hole at its edge.

Learn It!

For more information about numbers, see page G-33.

Numbers

Spell out numbers that can be expressed in one or two words, like *twelve* and *one hundred*.

Use a hyphen with numbers from twenty-one to ninety-nine.

Spell out ordinal numbers, like *first* and *second*.

Ordinal numbers tell the order or position in a sequence.

Fix It! Place a line through the incorrect number and write the correct word above it.

Timmy met ~~9~~ *nine* other mice on the ~~2nd~~ *second* day.

Comma

A **comma** is used to separate items in a sentence. Week 5 you learned two comma rules to use with coordinating conjunctions: a and b; a, b, and c.

Find It! Find the coordinating conjunction. Count how many items it connects.

Fix It! Add commas to separate three or more items in a series.

The cook opened (v) the basket**,** saw (v) Timmy**,** and (cc) screamed (v).

Ask students to identify the coordinating conjunction and explain what it connects. If it connects three or more items, commas must be used.

And connects three verbs: *opened*, *saw*, *screamed*. Use two commas. a, b, and c

Think About It!

Week 5 you learned that coordinating conjunctions (cc) are used to connect items. If the cc connects two items in a series, you should not use a comma. However, if the cc connects three or more items, you must use a comma.

Two Items: The cook grabbed the broom and stomped her foot.

In this sentence *and* connects *grabbed* and *stomped*.
Do not use a comma to separate two verbs.

Three Items: The cook grabbed the broom, stomped her foot, and jumped on the chair.

In this sentence *and* connects *grabbed, stomped,* and *jumped*.
Use two commas to separate three verbs.

Four Items: The cook grabbed the broom, stomped her foot, jumped on the chair, and yelled for help.

In this sentence *and* connects *grabbed, stomped, jumped,* and *yelled*.
Use three commas to separate four verbs.

Can you think of a fifth thing the cook may have done? If you wrote a sentence in which *and* connected five verbs, how many commas would be needed?

The cook may have fainted on the spot.

Use four commas to separate five verbs.

Read It!	Mark It!	Fix It!
he dropped onto a wooden table. it was set for 10 mice. the glasses platters and plates **shattered**	2 articles (ar)	3 capitals
	5 nouns (n)	2 commas
	2 pronouns (pr)	1 end mark
	2 adjectives (adj)	1 number
shattered broke into many pieces	1 coordinating conjunction (cc)	
	2 prepositional phrases	
	3 subject-verb pairs (s v)	

Day 1

s pr he v dropped onto ar a adj wooden n table. s pr it v was v set for adj ten ~~10~~ n mice.

ar the s n glasses, s n platters, cc and s n plates v **shattered.**

Capitalization	***He***; ***It***; ***The*** first word of the sentence
End Marks	Use a period at the end of a statement.
Pronoun	***He*** replaces *Timmy* ***It*** replaces *table.*
Adjective	What kind of table? ***wooden*** How many mice? ***ten***
S V Pairs	***He dropped***; ***It was set***; ***glasses, platters, plates shattered***
Commas	Use commas to separate three or more items in a series connected with a coordinating conjunction. **PATTERN a, b, and c** *glasses*, *platters*, and *plates*

Rewrite It! He dropped onto a wooden table. It was set for ten mice. The glasses, platters, and plates shattered.

Read It!	Mark It!	Fix It!
"who is this" asked johnny curiously. johnny was an important town mouse "i am timmy," squeaked the **newcomer**	2 articles (ar) 5 nouns (n) 1 pronoun (pr) 2 adjectives (adj) 5 subject-verb pairs (s v)	5 capitals 3 end marks

newcomer
someone who has newly arrived

"who is this**?**" asked johnny curiously. johnny was an important town mouse**.**

"i am timmy," squeaked the **newcomer.**

Capitalization	***Who*** first word of the quoted sentence ***Johnny*** proper noun ***Johnny*** proper noun; first word of the sentence ***I*** personal pronoun I; first word of the quoted sentence ***Timmy*** proper noun
End Marks	Use a question mark at the end of a question. Place it inside the closing quotation mark. Use a period at the end of a statement.
Pronoun	***I*** replaces *Timmy*
Adjective	What kind of mouse? ***town*** What kind of town mouse? ***important***
S V Pairs	***Who is***; ***Johnny asked***; ***Johnny was***; ***I am***; ***newcomer squeaked***
Note	In the first sentence *Who* does not start a *who/which* clause. *Who* begins a question.

Rewrite It!

"Who is this?" asked Johnny curiously. Johnny was an important town mouse.

"I am Timmy," squeaked the newcomer.

Read It! | **Mark It!** | **Fix It!**

the unknown visitor had surprised johnny, who quickly **recalled** his manners

recalled
remembered

1 article (ar)
3 nouns (n)
2 adjectives (adj)
1 *who/which* clause (w/w)
2 subject-verb pairs (s v)

2 capitals
1 end mark

the unknown visitor had surprised johnny,

(who quickly **recalled** his manners).

Capitalization	***The*** first word of the sentence ***Johnny*** proper noun
End Marks	Use a period at the end of a statement.
Adjective	What kind of visitor? ***unknown*** Whose manners? ***his*** The possessive pronoun *his* functions as an adjective.
W/W Clause	***who quickly recalled his manners*** describes *Johnny*
S V Pairs	***visitor had surprised***; ***who recalled***

Rewrite It! The unknown visitor had surprised Johnny, who quickly recalled his manners.

Read It!	Mark It!	Fix It!
with great politeness he introduced timmy two 9 other mice, who sat calmly with their **lengthy** tails neckties and jackets **lengthy** very long	6 nouns (n) 1 pronoun (pr) 5 adjectives (adj) 1 coordinating conjunction (cc) 3 prepositional phrases 1 *who/which* clause (w/w) 2 subject-verb pairs (s v)	2 capitals 2 commas 1 end mark 1 homophone 1 number

with great politeness he introduced timmy ~~two~~ to
~~9~~ nine other mice, (who sat calmly with their
lengthy tails, neckties, and jackets).

Capitalization	***With*** first word of the sentence ***Timmy*** proper noun
End Marks	Use a period at the end of a statement.
Pronoun	***he*** replaces *Johnny*
Adjective	What kind of politeness? ***great*** Which mice? ***other*** How many other mice? ***nine*** What kind of tails? ***lengthy*** Whose lengthy tails, neckties, and jackets? ***their*** The possessive pronoun *their* functions as an adjective.
W/W Clause	***who sat calmly with their lengthy tails, neckties, and jackets*** describes *mice*
S V Pairs	***he introduced***; ***who sat***
Commas	Use commas to separate three or more items in a series connected with a coordinating conjunction. **PATTERN a, b, and c** *tails*, *neckties*, and *jackets*
Homophones	Use ***to***, the preposition.

Rewrite It! With great politeness he introduced Timmy to nine other mice, who sat calmly with their lengthy tails, neckties, and jackets.

Learn It!

Adverb

An **adverb** modifies a verb, an adjective, or another adverb.

An adverb tells how, when, where, why, to what extent.

Memorize It! **how? when? where? why? to what extent?**

An adverb often ends in -ly.

Mark It! Write *ly* above each -ly adverb.

ly *ly*
Timmy recently ate an unusually large tomato.

For more information about adverbs, see page G-15.

Ask students to find verbs, adjectives, or adverbs and then ask questions to identify adverbs.

Ate when? ***recently***
recently modifies a verb (ate)

Large to what extent? ***unusually***
unusually modifies an adjective (large)

-ly Adverb

An **-ly adverb** dresses up writing when it creates a strong image or feeling. Look for -ly adverbs in this book and write them on the -ly Adverb collection page, Appendix II.

Not all adverbs end in -ly, such as *not*, *sometimes*, and *here*, *there*, and *soon*. In this book, students only mark -ly adverbs.

Adjective

An **adjective** describes a noun or pronoun.

An adjective tells which one, what kind, how many, or whose.

Week 6 you learned that an adjective usually comes before the word it describes. An adjective that describes a subject may follow a linking verb.

The scared mice ran.

An adjective usually comes before the word it describes. The adjective *scared* describes *mice*. What kind of mice? *scared*

The mice were scared.

An adjective may follow a linking verb. The linking verb (were) links the subject (mice) to an adjective (scared). The adjective *scared* describes *mice*. What kind of mice? *scared*

Capitalization

Capitalize proper adjectives formed from proper nouns.

Timmy's tail bumped the English teacup.

The proper adjective *Timmy's* comes from the proper noun *Timmy,* the name of a specific person. The proper adjective *English* comes from the proper noun *England,* the name of a specific country.

Think About It!

Many words can be used as different parts of speech. However, a word can perform only one part of speech at a time. For example, *light* can be a noun, adjective, or verb.

Noun: The light hurt my eyes.

In this sentence *light* is a thing.
A noun is a person, place, thing, or idea.

Adjective: The light rain was falling.

In this sentence *light* describes rain. What kind of rain? *light.*
An adjective describes a noun or pronoun.

Verb: The lamps light the room.

In this sentence *light* is a verb. *Light* is the action. What *light* the room? *lamps.* The subject-verb pair is *lamps light.*

Read It!	Mark It!	Fix It!
in comparison, timmy's vest, which he usually wore outdoors, was **rumpled**, and dull	2 nouns (n) 1 pronoun (pr) 3 adjectives (adj) 1 -ly adverb (ly) 1 coordinating conjunction (cc) 1 prepositional phrase 1 *who/which* clause (w/w) 2 subject-verb pairs (s v)	2 capitals 1 comma 1 end mark

rumpled
wrinkled

in comparison, timmy's vest, (which he usually wore outdoors), was **rumpled**, and dull.

Capitalization	***In*** first word of the sentence ***Timmy's*** proper adjective
End Marks	Use a period at the end of a statement.
Pronoun	***he*** replaces *Timmy*
Adjective	Whose vest? ***Timmy's*** The dual adjectives *rumpled* and *dull* follow the linking verb and describe the subject (vest). What kind of vest? ***rumpled*** and ***dull***
-ly Adverb	Wore when? ***usually***
W/W Clause	***which he usually wore outdoors*** describes *vest*
S V Pairs	***vest was***; ***he wore***
Commas	Do not use a comma to separate two items connected with a coordinating conjunction. **PATTERN a and b** *rumpled* and *dull*

Rewrite It! In comparison, Timmy's vest, which he usually wore outdoors, was rumpled and dull.

Read It!	Mark It!	Fix It! Day 2
johnny kindly **invited** him too join them. they set an 11th plate, cup and napkin	1 article (ar) 4 nouns (n) 3 pronouns (pr) 1 adjective (adj) 1 -ly adverb (ly) 1 coordinating conjunction (cc) 2 subject-verb pairs (s v)	2 capitals 1 comma 1 end mark 1 homophone 1 number

invited
requested to come or join in

s n johnny ly kindly v **invited** pr him ~~too~~ to join pr them. s pr they v set ar an ~~11th~~ adj eleventh n plate, n cup, cc and n napkin.

Capitalization	***Johnny*** proper noun; first word of the sentence ***They*** first word of the sentence
End Marks	Use a period at the end of a statement.
Pronoun	***him*** replaces *Timmy* ***them***; ***They*** replace *mice*
Adjective	Which plate, cup, and napkin? ***eleventh***
-ly Adverb	Invited how? ***kindly***
S V Pairs	***Johnny invited***; ***They set***
Commas	Use commas to separate three or more items in a series connected with a coordinating conjunction. **PATTERN a, b, and c** *plate*, *cup*, **and** *napkin*
Homophones	Use ***to***, the infinitive marker.
Note	The phrase to *join* does not follow the **PATTERN preposition + noun (no verb)**. When *to* is followed by a verb, it is called an infinitive. Do not mark infinitives as prepositional phrases. Do not mark them as verbs. They function as neither.

Rewrite It! Johnny kindly invited him to join them. They set an eleventh plate, cup, and napkin.

Read It!	Mark It!	Fix It!
the **elegant** feast included 8 courses, which were served two the mice on 1 plate at a time	3 articles (ar)	1 capital
	5 nouns (n)	1 end mark
	3 adjectives (adj)	1 homophone
	1 *who/which* clause (w/w)	2 numbers
elegant fancy; grand	3 prepositional phrases	
	2 subject-verb pairs (s v)	

ar adj s n v adj eight n w/w s v

the **elegant** feast included ~~8~~ courses, (which were

v to ar n adj one n ar n

served ~~two~~ the mice on ~~1~~ plate at a time).

Capitalization	***The*** first word of the sentence
End Marks	Use a period at the end of a statement.
Adjective	What kind of feast? ***elegant*** How many courses? ***eight*** How many plates? ***one***
W/W Clause	***which were served to the mice on one plate at a time*** describes *courses*
S V Pairs	***feast included***; ***which were served***
Homophones	Use ***to***, the preposition.

Rewrite It! The elegant feast included eight courses, which were served to the mice on one plate at a time.

Read It!	Mark It!	Fix It!
the city food was **unfamiliar** too timmy, who normally avoided fancy dishes	1 article (ar)	2 capitals
	3 nouns (n)	1 end mark
	3 adjectives (adj)	1 homophone
	1 -ly adverb (ly)	
unfamiliar	1 prepositional phrase	
strange	1 *who/which* clause (w/w)	
	2 subject-verb pairs (s v)	

ar *adj* *s n* *v* *adj* *to* *n* *s w/w* *ly* *v* *adj* *n*

the city food was **unfamiliar** ~~too~~ timmy, **(**who normally avoided fancy dishes**).**

Capitalization	***The*** first word of the sentence ***Timmy*** proper noun
End Marks	Use a period at the end of a statement.
Adjective	What kind of food? ***city*** The adjective *unfamiliar* follows the linking verb and describes the subject (food). What kind of food? ***unfamiliar*** What kind of dishes? ***fancy***
-ly Adverb	Avoided when? ***normally***
W/W Clause	***who normally avoided fancy dishes*** describes *Timmy*
S V Pairs	***food was***; ***who avoided***
Homophones	Use ***to***, the preposition.

Rewrite It! The city food was unfamiliar to Timmy, who normally avoided fancy dishes.

Learn It!

That Clause

A ***that* clause** is a group of words that begins with the word *that* and contains a subject and a verb. It must be added to a sentence that is already complete.

For more information about *that* clauses, see page G-41.

Mark It! Place parentheses around the *that* clause and write **that** above the word *that*. Write **v** above each verb and **s** above each subject.

that **s** **v**
Timmy knew **(**that the cat ate mice**)**.

Ask students to identify the subject and verb in the *that* clause.

What is the verb? ***ate***

What ate? ***cat***

 *That* clauses do not take commas.

Contraction

A **contraction** combines two words into one. It uses an apostrophe to show where a letter or letters have been removed.

For more information about contractions, see page G-28.

cannot ⟶ can**'**t	The **'** shows where *no* has been removed.
could not ⟶ couldn**'**t	The **'** shows where *o* has been removed.
did not ⟶ didn**'**t	The **'** shows where *o* has been removed.
do not ⟶ don**'**t	The **'** shows where *o* has been removed.
he had ⟶ he**'**d	The **'** shows where *ha* has been removed.
he would ⟶ he**'**d	The **'** shows where *woul* has been removed.
it is ⟶ it**'**s	The **'** shows where *i* has been removed.
she will ⟶ she**'**ll	The **'** shows where *wi* has been removed.
they are ⟶ they**'**re	The **'** shows where *a* has been removed.
was not ⟶ wasn**'**t	The **'** shows where *o* has been removed.

Fix It! Place an apostrophe to show where a letter or letters have been removed.

Don**'**t be afraid of the cat.

Ask students to identify what letter has been removed.

The apostrophe shows where the letter **o** has been removed from the phrase *Do not*.

Think About It!

Many words can be used as different parts of speech. However, a word can perform only one part of speech at a time. For example, *meeting* can be a verb, adjective, or noun.

Verb: The mice were meeting in the kitchen.

In this sentence *meeting* is a verb because it follows the helping verb *were*. A word that ends in -ing functions as a verb only if it follows a helping verb.

Adjective: The mice gathered in the meeting room.

In this sentence *meeting* describes room. What kind of room? *meeting*. An adjective describes a noun or pronoun.

Noun: The mice agreed to have a meeting.

In this sentence *meeting* is a thing. A noun is a person, place, thing, or idea.

Read It!	Mark It!	Fix It! Day 1
he didnt want to join them, but he **recognized** that hed seem terribly rude	4 pronouns (pr) 1 adjective (adj) 1 -ly adverb (ly) 1 coordinating conjunction (cc) 1 *that* clause (that) 3 subject-verb pairs (s v)	1 capital 1 end mark 2 apostrophes

recognized
realized as true

s pr he *v* didn't *v* want to join *pr* them, *cc* but *s pr* he *v* **recognized**

that (that *s pr* he'd *v* seem terribly *ly* rude *adj*).

Capitalization	***He*** first word of the sentence
End Marks	Use a period at the end of a statement.
Pronoun	***He*** replaces *Timmy* ***them*** replaces *mice* ***he; he*** replace *Timmy*
Adjective	The adjective *rude* follows the linking verb and describes the subject (he). What kind of he (Timmy)? ***rude***
-ly Adverb	Rude to what extent? ***terribly***
S V Pairs	***He did want***; ***he recognized***; ***he'd seem*** The contraction *didn't* includes both a helping verb (did) and an adverb (not). The contraction *he'd* includes both a subject (he) and a helping verb (would).
Note	The phrase *to join* does not follow the **PATTERN preposition + noun (no verb)**. When *to* is followed by a verb, it is called an infinitive. Do not mark infinitives as prepositional phrases. Do not mark them as verbs. They function as neither.

Rewrite It! He didn't want to join them, but he recognized that he'd seem terribly rude.

Read It!	Mark It!	Fix It!
sadly, the noise, which made timmy **jittery**, didnt stop. he dropped a plate, and a spoon	3 articles (ar) 4 nouns (n) 1 pronoun (pr) 1 adjective (adj) 1 -ly adverb (ly) 1 coordinating conjunction (cc) 1 *who/which* clause (w/w) 3 subject-verb pairs (s v)	3 capitals 1 comma 1 end mark 1 apostrophe

jittery
very nervous; jumpy

sadly, the noise, (which made timmy **jittery**), didn't stop. he dropped a plate, and a spoon.

Capitalization	***Sadly***; ***He*** first word of the sentence ***Timmy*** proper noun
End Marks	Use a period at the end of a statement.
Pronoun	***He*** replaces *Timmy*
Adjective	What kind of Timmy? ***jittery***
-ly Adverb	The noise didn't stop how? ***Sadly*** *Sadly* is a sentence adverb. It modifies the entire sentence: it was sad that the noise didn't stop. For this reason, it doesn't answer a question about the verb but about the entire sentence. It requires a comma.
W/W Clause	***which made Timmy jittery*** describes *noise*
S V Pairs	***noise did stop***; ***which made***; ***He dropped*** The contraction *didn't* includes both a helping verb (did) and an adverb (not).
Commas	Do not use a comma to separate two items connected with a coordinating conjunction. **PATTERN a and b** *plate* and *spoon*

Rewrite It! Sadly, the noise, which made Timmy jittery, didn't stop. He dropped a plate and a spoon.

Read It!	Mark It!	Fix It! Day 3
johnny, who wanted to be a kind mouse, **hastily** said, "you dont need to worry. they arent our plates"	1 article (ar) 3 nouns (n) 2 pronouns (pr) 2 adjectives (adj) 1 -ly adverb (ly) 1 *who/which* clause (w/w) 4 subject-verb pairs (s v)	3 capitals 1 end mark 2 apostrophes

hastily
speedily; quickly

johnny, (who wanted to be a kind mouse), **hastily** said, "you don't need to worry. they aren't our plates."

Capitalization	***Johnny*** proper noun; first word of the sentence ***You***; ***They*** first word of the quoted sentence
End Marks	Use a period at the end of a statement. Place it inside the closing quotation mark.
Pronoun	***You*** replaces *Timmy* ***They*** replaces *plates*
Adjective	What kind of mouse? ***kind*** Whose plates? ***our*** The possessive pronoun *our* functions as an adjective.
-ly Adverb	Said how? ***hastily***
W/W Clause	***who wanted to be a kind mouse*** describes *Johnny*
S V Pairs	***Johnny said***; ***who wanted***; ***You do need***; ***They are*** The contraction *don't* includes both a helping verb (do) and an adverb (not). The contraction *aren't* includes both a helping verb (are) and an adverb (not). *To be* and *to worry* are infinitives. They do not function as a verb.

Rewrite It! Johnny, who wanted to be a kind mouse, hastily said, "You don't need to worry. They aren't our plates."

Read It!	Mark It!	Fix It!
timmy saw that the to youngest mice had **scurried** upstairs	1 article (ar) 2 nouns (n) 2 adjectives (adj) 1 *that* clause (that) 2 subject-verb pairs (s v)	1 capital 1 end mark 1 homophone

scurried
moved quickly

s n *v* *that* *ar* *adj two* *adj* *s n*

timmy saw (that the ~~to~~ two youngest mice

v *v*

had **scurried** upstairs).

Capitalization	***Timmy*** proper noun; first word of the sentence
End Marks	Use a period at the end of a statement.
Adjective	Which mice? ***youngest*** How many youngest mice? ***two***
S V Pairs	***Timmy saw***; ***mice had scurried***
Homophones	Use ***two***, the number.

Rewrite It! Timmy saw that the two youngest mice had scurried upstairs.

Review It!

Preposition

A **preposition** starts a phrase that shows the relationship between a noun or pronoun and another word in the sentence.

Answer the following questions:

What is the prepositional phrase pattern? preposition + noun (no verb)

List ten prepositions. Prepositions are listed on page 13.

Why is this a prepositional phrase? after the dinner
It starts with a preposition (after) and ends with a noun (dinner). It has an article in between but no verb.

Why is this not a prepositional phrase? after they ate dinner
It has a verb (ate).

Fill in the blanks with prepositions. There are multiple right answers.

The maid walked __into__ the kitchen. Every morning she drank coffee __with__ milk. Then she took eggs and bacon __from__ the refrigerator. She made breakfast __in__ a pan __on__ the stove. The mice watched the maid __from__ a distance. When the maid left the room, the mice scurried __up__ the chairs and __onto__ the counters. They hunted __for__ crumbs __throughout__ the kitchen.

Encourage students to have fun with this exercise. The goal is to become familiar with prepositions.

There are multiple right answers for each blank. For example, prepositions *around*, *by*, *through* could also be used in the first blank.

Read It!	Mark It!	Fix It! Day 1
they returned with food for the table. for several minutes they **gasped** for breath	1 article (ar)	2 capitals
	4 nouns (n)	1 end mark
	2 pronouns (pr)	
	1 adjective (adj)	
gasped struggled for breath with mouth open	4 prepositional phrases	
	2 subject-verb pairs (s v)	

they returned with food for the table. for several minutes they **gasped** for breath.

Capitalization	***They***; ***For*** first word of the sentence
End Marks	Use a period at the end of a statement.
Pronoun	***They***; ***they*** replace *mice*
Adjective	How many minutes? ***several***
S V Pairs	***They returned***; ***they gasped***

Rewrite It! They returned with food for the table. For several minutes they gasped for breath.

Read It!	Mark It!	Fix It!
timmy **discovered** that they had been chased by the cat, who was constantly looking for mice	1 article (ar)	1 capital
	3 nouns (n)	1 end mark
	1 pronoun (pr)	
	1 -ly adverb (ly)	
discovered learned; found out	2 prepositional phrases	
	1 *who/which* clause (w/w)	
	1 *that* clause (that)	
	3 subject-verb pairs (s v)	

timmy **discovered** (that they had been chased by the cat), (who was constantly looking for mice).

Capitalization	***Timmy*** proper noun; first word of the sentence
End Marks	Use a period at the end of a statement.
Pronoun	***they*** replaces *mice*
-ly Adverb	Was looking when? ***constantly***
W/W Clause	***who was constantly looking for mice*** describes *cat*
S V Pairs	***Timmy discovered***; ***they had been chased***; ***who was looking*** In this sentence *looking* functions as a verb because it follows the helping verb *was*. A word that ends in -ing functions as a verb only if it follows a helping verb.

Rewrite It! Timmy discovered that they had been chased by the cat, who was constantly looking for mice.

Read It!	Mark It!	Fix It!
timmy squeaked **shrilly**. he feared that they would be hurt, or killed. he was scared	1 noun (n) 3 pronouns (pr) 1 adjective (adj) 1 -ly adverb (ly) 1 coordinating conjunction (cc) 1 *that* clause (that) 4 subject-verb pairs (s v)	3 capitals 1 comma 1 end mark

shrilly
with a sharp, high-pitched sound

timmy squeaked **shrilly**. he feared **(**that they would be hurt, or killed**)**. he was scared**.**

Capitalization	***Timmy*** proper noun; first word of the sentence ***He***; ***He*** first word of the sentence
End Marks	Use a period at the end of a statement.
Pronoun	***He***; ***He*** replace *Timmy* ***they*** replaces *mice*
Adjective	The adjective *scared* follows the linking verb and describes the subject (He). What kind of he (Timmy)? ***scared***
-ly Adverb	Squeaked how? ***shrilly***
S V Pairs	***Timmy squeaked***; ***He feared***; ***they would be hurt***, ***killed***; ***He was***
Commas	Do not use a comma to separate two items connected with a coordinating conjunction. **PATTERN a and b** *hurt* or *killed*

Rewrite It! Timmy squeaked shrilly. He feared that they would be hurt or killed. He was scared.

Read It!	Mark It!	Fix It!
johnny **calmly** said, "youve not eaten much food. would you like cold milk, and a biscuit with jelly"	1 article (ar)	3 capitals
	5 nouns (n)	1 comma
	2 pronouns (pr)	1 end mark
	2 adjectives (adj)	1 apostrophe
calmly without worry or excitement	1 -ly adverb (ly)	
	1 coordinating conjunction (cc)	
	1 prepositional phrase	
	3 subject-verb pairs (s v)	

johnny **calmly** said, "you've not eaten much food. would you like cold milk, and a biscuit with jelly?"

Capitalization	***Johnny*** proper noun; first word of the sentence ***You've***; ***Would*** first word of the quoted sentence
End Marks	Use a question mark at the end of a question. Place it inside the closing quotation mark.
Pronoun	***You***; ***you*** replace *Timmy*
Adjective	How much food? ***much*** *How much* is a form of the adjective question *how many*. What kind of milk? ***cold***
-ly Adverb	Said how? ***calmly***
S V Pairs	***Johnny said***; ***You've eaten***; ***you Would like*** The contraction *You've* includes both a subject (You) and a helping verb (have).
Commas	Do not use a comma to separate two items connected with a coordinating conjunction. **PATTERN a and b** *milk* and *biscuit*

Rewrite It! Johnny calmly said, "You've not eaten much food. Would you like cold milk and a biscuit with jelly?"

Learn It!

Homophone

A **homophone** is a word that sounds like another word but is spelled differently and has a different meaning. Correctly use the homophones *your* and *you're*.

Your is a possessive pronoun: *your tail* (the tail belongs to you).

The possessive pronoun *your* tells whose and functions as an adjective.

You're is a contraction: *you're early* (you are early).

The contraction *you're* is a shortened form of *you are* and functions as the subject pronoun (you) and verb (are) of the clause.

Fix It! Place a line through the incorrect homophone and write the correct word above it.

Mark It! If the correct homophone is *your*, write ***adj*** above *your*. If the correct homophone is *you're*, write ***pr*** and ***s*** above *you*. Write ***v*** above *'re*.

s v
pr *adj*
You're *your*
~~Your~~ not sleeping in ~~you're~~ bed!

For more information about impostor -ly adverbs, see page G-37.

Impostor -ly Adverb

An **impostor -ly adverb** is a word that looks like an -ly adverb because it ends in -ly but is actually an adjective.

If the -ly word modifies a verb, adjective, or adverb, it will tell when, where, why, how, to what extent. It is an adverb.

If the -ly word describes a noun or pronoun, it will tell which one or what kind. It is an adjective.

Mark It! Write ***ly*** above each -ly adverb. Write ***adj*** above each adjective.

adj *ly*
The ugly cat boldly stalked the mice.

Ask students to identify the -ly word and determine if it is an adverb or an impostor (adjective).

What kind of cat? ***ugly*** *Ugly* answers what kind and describes a noun, so *ugly* is an adjective.

Stalked how? ***boldly*** *Boldly* answers how and modifies a verb, so *boldly* is an adverb.

Common Impostors
These -ly words are adjectives.

chilly	holy	lovely	queenly
friendly	kingly	lowly	ugly
ghastly	knightly	orderly	worldly
ghostly	lonely	prickly	wrinkly

Noun of Direct Address

A **noun of direct address** (NDA) is a noun used to refer to someone directly. It names the person spoken to.

It can appear at any natural pause in a quoted sentence.

If you remove the NDA from the sentence, you will still have a sentence.

"Timmy**,** after dinner we can read books," Johnny said.

"After dinner**,** Timmy**,** we can read books," Johnny said.

"After dinner we can read books**,** Timmy," Johnny said.

Because a noun can perform only one function in a sentence, a noun of direct address is never the subject of a sentence. In these sentences the noun of direct address is *Timmy* because that is the noun used to directly address the mouse. The subject is the pronoun *we*.

Comma

A **comma** is used to separate items in a sentence. Commas are used to separate the noun of direct address from the rest of the sentence.

Place commas around a noun of direct address.

Ask students to identify the noun of direct address.

Johnny is the noun of direct address. Place a comma after *Johnny*.

Fix It! Add commas to separate the noun of direct address from the sentence.

"Johnny**,** where are you going?" the little mouse asked.

Read It!	Mark It!	Fix It! Day 1
timmy politely answered, "johnny i am too **nervous** to eat you're food"	3 nouns (n) 1 pronoun (pr) 2 adjectives (adj) 1 -ly adverb (ly) 2 subject-verb pairs (s v)	3 capitals 1 comma 1 end mark 1 homophone

nervous
excitable and worried

timmy (s, n) politely (ly) answered (v), "johnny (n), i (s, pr) am (v) too **nervous** (adj) to eat ~~you're~~ your (adj) food (n)."

Capitalization	***Timmy*** proper noun; first word of the sentence ***Johnny*** proper noun; first word of the quoted sentence ***I*** personal pronoun I
End Marks	Use a period at the end of a statement. Place it inside the closing quotation mark.
Pronoun	***I*** replaces *Timmy*
Adjective	The adjective *nervous* follows the linking verb and describes the subject (I). What kind of I (Timmy)? ***nervous*** Whose food? ***your*** The possessive pronoun *your* functions as an adjective.
-ly Adverb	Answered how? ***politely***
S V Pairs	***Timmy answered***; ***I am*** *To eat* is an infinitive. It does not function as a verb.
Commas	Place commas around a noun of direct address (NDA). ***Johnny,***
Homophones	Use ***your***, the possessive pronoun.

Rewrite It! Timmy politely answered, "Johnny, I am too nervous to eat your food."

Read It!	Mark It!	Fix It!
"timmy your not eating. maybe you should go to bed," johnny quietly **suggested**	3 nouns (n)	3 capitals
	2 pronouns (pr)	1 comma
	1 -ly adverb (ly)	1 end mark
	1 prepositional phrase	1 homophone
	3 subject-verb pairs (s v)	

suggested
proposed an idea for someone to think about

"timmy, ~~your~~ you're not eating. maybe you should go to bed," johnny quietly **suggested.**

Capitalization	***Timmy*** proper noun; first word of the quoted sentence ***Maybe*** first word of the quoted sentence ***Johnny*** proper noun
End Marks	Use a period at the end of a statement.
Pronoun	***you***; ***you*** replace *Timmy*
-ly Adverb	Suggested how? ***quietly***
S V Pairs	***you're eating***; ***you should go***; ***Johnny suggested*** The contraction *you're* includes both a subject (you) and a helping verb (are).
Commas	Place commas around a noun of direct address (NDA). ***Timmy,***
Homophones	Use ***you're***, the contraction for *you are.*

Rewrite It! "Timmy, you're not eating. Maybe you should go to bed," Johnny quietly suggested.

Read It!	Mark It!	Fix It! Day 3
they immediately went too a room upstairs. johnny offered timmy an ugly pillow, which looked **comfortable**	2 articles (ar) 4 nouns (n) 1 pronoun (pr) 2 adjectives (adj) 1 -ly adverb (ly) 1 prepositional phrase 1 *who/which* clause (w/w) 3 subject-verb pairs (s v)	3 capitals 1 end mark 1 homophone

comfortable
giving physical comfort or ease

they immediately went ~~too~~ to a room upstairs.

johnny offered timmy an ugly pillow, (which looked **comfortable**).

Capitalization	***They*** first word of the sentence ***Johnny*** proper noun; first word of the sentence ***Timmy*** proper noun
End Marks	Use a period at the end of a statement.
Pronoun	***They*** replaces *Timmy* and *Johnny*
Adjective	What kind of pillow? ***ugly*** The adjective *comfortable* follows the linking verb and describes the subject (which). What kind of which (pillow)? ***comfortable***
-ly Adverb	Went when? ***immediately***
W/W Clause	***which looked comfortable*** describes *pillow* The relative pronoun *which* replaces the noun *pillow*.
S V Pairs	***They went***; ***Johnny offered***; ***which looked***
Homophones	Use ***to***, the preposition.

Rewrite It! They immediately went to a room upstairs. Johnny offered Timmy an ugly pillow, which looked comfortable.

Read It!	Mark It!	Fix It! Day 4
timmy **reluctantly** sniffed the neat clean and unused pillow. it's wrinkly cover smelled like a cat	2 articles (ar)	2 capitals
	4 nouns (n)	2 commas
	5 adjectives (adj)	1 end mark
	1 -ly adverb (ly)	1 homophone
reluctantly unwillingly	1 coordinating conjunction (cc)	
	1 prepositional phrase	
	2 subject-verb pairs (s v)	

s n timmy ly **reluctantly** v sniffed ar the adj neat**,** adj clean**,** cc and adj unused n pillow. adj Its ~~it's~~ adj wrinkly s n cover v smelled like ar a n cat**.**

Capitalization	***Timmy*** proper noun; first word of the sentence ***Its*** first word of the sentence
End Marks	Use a period at the end of a statement.
Adjective	What kind of pillow? ***neat***, ***clean***, and ***unused*** What kind of cover? ***wrinkly*** Whose wrinkly cover? ***its*** The possessive pronoun *its* functions as an adjective.
S V Pairs	***Timmy sniffed***; ***cover smelled***
Commas	Use commas to separate three or more items in a series connected with a coordinating conjunction. **PATTERN a, b, and c** *neat, clean,* and *unused*
Homophones	Use ***Its***, the possessive pronoun.

Rewrite It! Timmy reluctantly sniffed the neat, clean, and unused pillow. Its wrinkly cover smelled like a cat.

Learn It!

Adverb Clause

An **adverb clause** is a group of words that begins with a www word and contains a subject and a verb. An adverb clause must be added to a sentence that is already complete.

Memorize It! **www word + subject + verb**

Use the acronym *www.asia.b* to learn the eight most common www words.

Memorize It!

w	*w*	*w*	*a*	*s*	*i*	*a*	*b*
when	**while**	**where**	**as**	**since**	**if**	**although**	**because**

Mark It! Place parentheses around the adverb clause and write *AC* above the www word. Write *v* above each verb and *s* above each subject.

(When[AC] the cat[s] prowled[v] at night), the mice hid (where[AC] he[s] could[v] not reach[v] them).

Use a comma after an adverb clause that comes before a main clause.
PATTERN AC, MC

Do not use a comma before an adverb clause.
PATTERN MC AC

Think About It!

Many words can be used as different parts of speech. However, a word can perform only one part of speech at a time. For example, *since* can be a preposition that begins a prepositional phrase, and *since* can be a www word that begins an adverb clause.

Prepositional Phrase: <u>Since his trip</u> Timmy slept poorly.

Since his trip is a prepositional phrase.
PATTERN preposition (since) + noun (trip) (no verb)

Adverb Clause: (Since he had traveled), Timmy slept poorly.

Since he had traveled is an adverb clause.
PATTERN www word (since) + subject (he) + verb (had traveled)

For more information about adverb clauses, see page G-21.

Ask students to identify the subject and verb in the adverb clause.

What is the verb? ***prowled***

What prowled? ***cat***
Use a comma after an adverb clause that comes before a main clause. AC, MC

What is the verb? ***could reach***

What could reach? ***he***
Do not use a comma before an adverb clause. MC AC

Draw students' attention to the comma patterns.

Require students to copy the commas correctly when they rewrite the passages.

There can function as other parts of speech, but in this book students will only see it as an adverb.

Homophone

A **homophone** is a word that sounds like another word but is spelled differently and has a different meaning. Correctly use the homophones *there, their,* and *they're.*

There is an adverb pointing to a place: *over there* (there is the spot).

Their is a possessive pronoun: *their tails* (the tails belong to them).

The possessive pronoun *their* tells whose and functions as an adjective.

They're is a contraction: *they're hungry* (they are hungry).

The contraction *they're* is a shortened form of *they are* and functions as the subject pronoun (they) and verb (are) of the clause.

Fix It! Place a line through the incorrect homophone and write the correct word above it.

Mark It! If the correct homophone is *their,* write ***adj*** above *their.*
If the correct homophone is *they're,* write ***pr*** and ***s*** above *they.*
Write ***v*** above *'re.*

adj / *their* — s v / pr / *they're*

The mice tuck in ~~there~~ tails because ~~their~~ too long.

Read It!	Mark It!	Fix It!
timmy fearfully wondered if catnap poked, and **prodded** the pillow at night	1 article (ar)	2 capitals
	4 nouns (n)	1 comma
	1 -ly adverb (ly)	1 end mark
	1 coordinating conjunction (cc)	
prodded	1 prepositional phrase	
jabbed or poked with something pointed	1 adverb clause (AC)	
	2 subject-verb pairs (s v)	

Day 1

timmy fearfully wondered (if catnap poked, and **prodded** the pillow at night).

Capitalization	***Timmy*** proper noun; first word of the sentence ***Catnap*** proper noun
End Marks	Use a period at the end of a statement.
-ly Adverb	Wondered how? ***fearfully***
S V Pairs	***Timmy wondered***; ***Catnap poked***, ***prodded***
Commas	Do not use a comma to separate two items connected with a coordinating conjunction. **PATTERN a and b** *poked* and *prodded*

Rewrite It! Timmy fearfully wondered if Catnap poked and prodded the pillow at night.

Read It!	Mark It!	Fix It!
since he feared the cat, he had **ghastly** dreams about cats with teeth, and claws	1 article (ar)	1 capital
	5 nouns (n)	1 comma
	2 pronouns (pr)	1 end mark
ghastly horrible; frightful	1 adjective (adj)	
	1 coordinating conjunction (cc)	
	2 prepositional phrases	
	1 adverb clause (AC)	
	2 subject-verb pairs (s v)	

AC (since *s pr* he *v* feared the *ar* cat *n*), he *s pr* had *v* **ghastly** *adj* dreams *n*

about cats *n* with teeth *n*, and *cc* claws *n*.

Capitalization	***Since*** first word of the sentence
End Marks	Use a period at the end of a statement.
Pronoun	***he***; ***he*** replace *Timmy*
Adjective	What kind of dreams? ***ghastly***
S V Pairs	***he feared***; ***he had***
Commas	Do not use a comma to separate two items connected with a coordinating conjunction. **PATTERN a and b** *teeth* and *claws*

Rewrite It! Since he feared the cat, he had ghastly dreams about cats with teeth and claws.

Read It! | **Mark It!** | **Fix It!** Day 3

when timmy awoke in the morning, the town mice **offered** him a fancy breakfast. it smelled good

offered
presented for acceptance or rejection

3 articles (ar)
4 nouns (n)
2 pronouns (pr)
3 adjectives (adj)
1 prepositional phrase
1 adverb clause (AC)
3 subject-verb pairs (s v)

3 capitals
1 end mark

(when timmy awoke in the morning), the town mice **offered** him a fancy breakfast. it smelled good.

Capitalization	***When***; ***It*** first word of the sentence ***Timmy*** proper noun
End Marks	Use a period at the end of a statement.
Pronoun	***him*** replaces *Timmy* ***it*** replaces *breakfast*
Adjective	Which mice? ***town*** What kind of breakfast? ***fancy*** The adjective *good* follows the linking verb and describes the subject (It). What kind of it (breakfast)? ***good***
S V Pairs	***Timmy awoke***; ***mice offered***; ***It smelled***

Rewrite It! When Timmy awoke in the morning, the town mice offered him a fancy breakfast. It smelled good.

Read It!	Mark It!	Fix It! Day 4
the mice, who enjoyed there food, proudly **boasted** that it was a dish with eggs in a cream sauce	3 articles (ar)	1 capital
	5 nouns (n)	1 end mark
	1 pronoun (pr)	1 homophone
	2 adjectives (adj)	
boasted spoke with too much pride; bragged	1 -ly adverb (ly)	
	2 prepositional phrases	
	1 *who/which* clause (w/w)	
	1 *that* clause (that)	
	3 subject-verb pairs (s v)	

ar *s n* *s w/w* *v* *adj their* *n* *ly* *v*

the mice, (who enjoyed ~~there~~ food), proudly **boasted**

that *s pr* *v* *ar* *n* *n* *ar* *adj* *n*

(that it was a dish with eggs in a cream sauce).

Capitalization	***The*** first word of the sentence
End Marks	Use a period at the end of a statement.
Pronoun	***it*** replaces *dish*
Adjective	Whose food? ***their*** The possessive pronoun *their* functions as an adjective. What kind of sauce? ***cream***
-ly Adverb	Boasted how? ***proudly***
W/W Clause	***who enjoyed their food*** describes *mice*
S V Pairs	***mice boasted***; ***who enjoyed***; ***it was***
Homophones	Use ***their***, the possessive pronoun.

Rewrite It! The mice, who enjoyed their food, proudly boasted that it was a dish with eggs in a cream sauce.

Review It!

Who/Which Clause, *That* Clause, and Adverb Clause

A *who/which* clause, a *that* clause, and an adverb clause add detail to a sentence.

Who/Which Clause

contains a subject and verb

is added to a sentence that is already complete

begins with the word *who* or *which*

usually uses commas

That Clause

contains a subject and verb

is added to a sentence that is already complete

begins with the word *that*

does not use commas

Adverb Clause

contains a subject and verb

is added to a sentence that is already complete

begins with a www word

uses a comma after but not before

Show students how these clauses are similar.

Each type of clause contains a subject and verb and is added to a sentence that is already complete.

Show students how these clauses are different.

Each type of clause begins with different words and has different comma rules.

The first word of the clause indicates what type of clause it is.

Complete this exercise orally. Change the sentence by adding different types of clauses. There are multiple right answers.

Encourage students to practice forming complex sentences orally. Students who can easily create oral sentences struggle less when writing.

The cook could not find the cheese.

The cook, who ____________, could not find the cheese.

The cook could not find the cheese that ____________.

The cook could not find the cheese when ____________.

The possibilities are endless. The cook, *who was fired; who saw the mouse; who forgot her glasses at home; who was responsible for making dinner,* could not find the cheese.

Substitute *while* or *where* for *when.*

Read It!	Mark It!	Fix It! Day 1
timmy couldnt easily **digest** there food because he needed fruit nuts, and beans from his garden	6 nouns (n)	1 capital
	1 pronoun (pr)	1 comma
	2 adjectives (adj)	1 end mark
	1 -ly adverb (ly)	1 homophone
digest	1 coordinating conjunction (cc)	1 apostrophe
break down food in the body	1 prepositional phrase	
	1 adverb clause (AC)	
	2 subject-verb pairs (s v)	

s n timmy *v* couldn't *ly* easily *v* **digest** ~~there~~ *adj* their *n* food *AC* (because *s pr* he *v* needed *n* fruit, *n* nuts, *cc* and *n* beans from *adj* his *n* garden).

Capitalization	***Timmy*** proper noun; first word of the sentence
End Marks	Use a period at the end of a statement.
Pronoun	***he*** replaces *Timmy*
Adjective	Whose food? ***their*** The possessive pronoun *their* functions as an adjective. Whose garden? ***his*** The possessive pronoun *his* functions as an adjective.
-ly Adverb	Couldn't digest how? ***easily***
S V Pairs	***Timmy could digest***; ***he needed*** The contraction *couldn't* includes both a helping verb (could) and an adverb (not).
Commas	Use commas to separate three or more items in a series connected with a coordinating conjunction. **PATTERN a, b, and c** *fruit, nuts,* and *beans*
Homophones	Use ***their***, the possessive pronoun.

Rewrite It! Timmy couldn't easily digest their food because he needed fruit, nuts, and beans from his garden.

Read It!	Mark It!	Fix It!
throughout the day loud noises, which never stopped, **disturbed** timmy. they seemed strange	1 article (ar) 3 nouns (n) 1 pronoun (pr) 2 adjectives (adj) 1 prepositional phrase 1 *who/which* clause (w/w) 3 subject-verb pairs (s v)	3 capitals 1 end mark

disturbed
troubled

throughout the day loud noises, (which never stopped), **disturbed** timmy. they seemed strange.

Capitalization	***Throughout***; ***They*** first word of the sentence ***Timmy*** proper noun
End Marks	Use a period at the end of a statement.
Pronoun	***They*** replaces *noises*
Adjective	What kind of noises? ***loud*** The adjective *strange* follows the linking verb and describes the subject (They). What kind of They (noises)? ***strange***
W/W Clause	***which never stopped*** describes *noises*
S V Pairs	***noises disturbed***; ***which stopped***; ***They seemed***

Rewrite It! Throughout the day loud noises, which never stopped, disturbed Timmy. They seemed strange.

Read It!	Mark It!	Fix It! Day 3
julia, and sarah pounded rugs in the afternoon while catnap **pestered** the canary in it's cage	2 articles (ar)	3 capitals
	7 nouns (n)	1 comma
	1 adjective (adj)	1 end mark
	1 coordinating conjunction (cc)	1 homophone
pestered bothered; irritated	2 prepositional phrases	
	1 adverb clause (AC)	
	2 subject-verb pairs (s v)	

julia, and sarah pounded rugs in the afternoon (while catnap **pestered** the canary in ~~it's~~ its cage).

Capitalization	***Julia*** proper noun; first word of the sentence ***Sarah***; ***Catnap*** proper noun
End Marks	Use a period at the end of a statement.
Adjective	Whose cage? ***its*** The possessive pronoun *its* functions as an adjective.
S V Pairs	***Julia, Sarah pounded***; ***Catnap pestered***
Commas	Do not use a comma to separate two items connected with a coordinating conjunction. **PATTERN a and b** *Julia* and *Sarah*
Homophones	Use ***its***, the possessive pronoun.

Rewrite It! Julia and Sarah pounded rugs in the afternoon while Catnap pestered the canary in its cage.

Read It!	Mark It!	Fix It!
during the evening the mice **wandered** through the house as they eagerly searched for tasty treats	3 articles (ar) 4 nouns (n) 1 pronoun (pr) 1 adjective (adj) 1 -ly adverb (ly) 3 prepositional phrases 1 adverb clause (AC) 2 subject-verb pairs (s v)	1 capital 1 end mark

wandered
walked around without purpose or direction

ar n ar s/n v
during the evening the mice **wandered** through

ar n AC s/pr ly v adj n
the house (as they eagerly searched for tasty treats).

Capitalization	***During*** first word of the sentence
End Marks	Use a period at the end of a statement.
Pronoun	***they*** replaces *mice*
Adjective	What kind of treats? ***tasty***
-ly Adverb	Searched how? ***eagerly***
S V Pairs	***mice wandered***; ***they searched***

Rewrite It! During the evening the mice wandered through the house as they eagerly searched for tasty treats.

Learn It!

Adverb Clause or Prepositional Phrase

These words usually begin adverb clauses.

when while where **as** **since** if although **because**

Pattern:
www word +
subject + verb

These words usually begin prepositional phrases.

aboard	around	between	in	opposite	toward
about	**as**	beyond	inside	out	under
above	at	by	instead of	outside	underneath
according to	**because of**	concerning	into	over	unlike
across	before	despite	like	past	until
after	behind	down	minus	regarding	unto
against	below	during	near	**since**	up, upon
along	beneath	except	of	through	with
amid	beside	for	off	throughout	within
among	besides	from	on, onto	to	without

Pattern:
preposition + noun
(no verb)

The words *as, since,* and *because* appear on both lists. When you mark the sentences, consider the patterns.

Adverb Clause: (As Johnny gave orders), the mice followed.

As Johnny gave orders is an adverb clause.
PATTERN www word (as) + subject (Johnny) + verb (gave)

The words *after*, *before*, and *until* are also www words that can begin adverb clauses.

Prepositional Phrase: As a leader Johnny took charge.

As a leader is a prepositional phrase.
PATTERN preposition (as) + noun (leader) (no verb)

The word *because* usually begins an adverb clause. However, when *because* is followed by *of*, the two words together are a preposition.

Adverb Clause: Johnny ate (because the food was tasty).

Because the food was tasty is an adverb clause.
PATTERN www word (because) + subject (food) + verb (was)

Prepositional Phrase: Johnny ate because of the tasty food.

Because of the tasty food is a prepositional phrase.
PATTERN preposition (because of) + noun (food) (no verb)

Read It!	Mark It!	Fix It! Day 1
at night timmy couldnt sleep because of the tall clock, which noisily **signaled** each hour	1 article (ar)	2 capitals
	4 nouns (n)	1 end mark
	2 adjectives (adj)	1 apostrophe
signaled gave a sign for; communicated	1 -ly adverb (ly)	
	2 prepositional phrases	
	1 *who/which* clause (w/w)	
	2 subject-verb pairs (s v)	

at night timmy couldn't sleep because of the tall clock, (which noisily **signaled** each hour).

(Markings: at night [n], timmy [s n], could [v], sleep [v], the [ar], tall [adj], clock [n], which [w/w, s], noisily [ly], signaled [v], each [adj], hour [n]; prepositional phrases underlined: at night; because of the tall clock)

Capitalization	***At*** first word of the sentence ***Timmy*** proper noun
End Marks	Use a period at the end of a statement.
Adjective	What kind of clock? ***tall*** Which hour? ***each***
-ly Adverb	Signaled how? ***noisily***
W/W Clause	***which noisily signaled each hour*** describes *clock*
S V Pairs	***Timmy could sleep***; ***which signaled*** The contraction *couldn't* includes both a helping verb (could) and an adverb (not).

Rewrite It! At night Timmy couldn't sleep because of the tall clock, which noisily signaled each hour.

Read It!	Mark It!	Fix It! Day 2
as time passed, timmy **longed** to return to his quiet, and peaceful home in the country	1 article (ar) 4 nouns (n) 3 adjectives (adj) 1 coordinating conjunction (cc) 2 prepositional phrases 1 adverb clause (AC) 2 subject-verb pairs (s v)	2 capitals 1 comma 1 end mark

longed
had a strong desire

(as time passed), timmy **longed** to return to his quiet, and peaceful home in the country.

Capitalization	***As*** first word of the sentence ***Timmy*** proper noun
End Marks	Use a period at the end of a statement.
Adjective	What kind of home? ***quiet*** and ***peaceful*** Whose quiet and peaceful home? ***his*** The possessive pronoun *his* functions as an adjective.
S V Pairs	***time passed***; ***Timmy longed*** *To return* is an infinitive. It does not function as a verb.
Commas	Do not use a comma to separate two items connected with a coordinating conjunction. **PATTERN a and b** *quiet* and *peaceful*

Rewrite It! As time passed, Timmy longed to return to his quiet and peaceful home in the country.

Read It!	Mark It!	Fix It! Day 3
in late may timmy **confessed** two johnny that he wanted to leave because he missed his home garden and friends	6 nouns (n)	4 capitals
	2 pronouns (pr)	2 commas
confessed admitted as true	2 adjectives (adj)	1 end mark
	1 coordinating conjunction (cc)	1 homophone
	2 prepositional phrases	
	1 *that* clause (that)	
	1 adverb clause (AC)	
	3 subject-verb pairs (s v)	

adj *n* *s n* *v* *to* *n* *that*

in late may timmy **confessed** ~~two~~ johnny **(**that

s pr *v* *AC* *s pr* *v* *adj* *n*

he wanted to leave**)** **(**because he missed his home**,**

n *cc* *n*

garden**,** and friends**).**

Capitalization	***In*** first word of the sentence ***May***; ***Timmy***; ***Johnny*** proper noun
End Marks	Use a period at the end of a statement.
Pronoun	***he***; ***he*** replace *Timmy*
Adjective	Which May? ***late*** Whose home, garden, and friends? ***his*** The possessive pronoun *his* functions as an adjective.
S V Pairs	***Timmy confessed***; ***he wanted***; ***he missed*** *To leave* is an infinitive. It does not function as a verb.
Commas	Use commas to separate three or more items in a series connected with a coordinating conjunction. **PATTERN a, b, and c** *home*, *garden*, and *friends*
Homophones	Use ***to***, the preposition.

Rewrite It! In late May Timmy confessed to Johnny that he wanted to leave because he missed his home, garden, and friends.

Read It!	Mark It!	Fix It!
"you miss your garden? i would never miss fruits, or vegetables," **remarked** johnny. "what did you do their"	4 nouns (n) 3 pronouns (pr) 1 adjective (adj) 1 coordinating conjunction (cc) 4 subject-verb pairs (s v)	4 capitals 1 comma 1 end mark 1 homophone

remarked
said casually; commented

"you miss your garden? i would never miss fruits, or vegetables," **remarked** johnny. "what did you do ~~their~~ there**?**"

Capitalization	***You***; ***What*** first word of the quoted sentence ***I*** personal pronoun I; first word of the quoted sentence ***Johnny*** proper noun
End Marks	Use a question mark at the end of a question. Place it inside the closing quotation mark.
Pronoun	***you*** replaces *Timmy* ***I*** replaces *Johnny* ***you*** replaces *Timmy*
Adjective	Whose garden? ***your*** The possessive pronoun *your* functions as an adjective.
S V Pairs	***You miss***; ***I would miss***; ***Johnny remarked***; ***you did do***
Commas	Do not use a comma to separate two items connected with a coordinating conjunction. **PATTERN a and b** *fruits* or *vegetables*
Homophones	Use ***there***, the adverb pointing to a place.

Rewrite It! "You miss your garden? I would never miss fruits or vegetables," remarked Johnny. "What did you do there?"

Learn It!

Possessive Adjective

An **adjective** describes a noun or pronoun.

An adjective tells which one, what kind, how many, or whose.

When a noun is followed by an apostrophe + s, it functions as a possessive adjective and shows ownership. It answers the question *whose.*

Timmy answered Johnny's question.

The noun *Johnny* is followed by an apostrophe + s. Because *Johnny's* functions as a possessive adjective, we call it an adjective, not a noun. Whose question? *Johnny's*

Without the apostrophe, the noun would be plural. There are not several *Johnnys* (plural).

Find It! Look for nouns that show ownership or possession. They will end in *s* and answer the question *whose.*

Fix It! Place an apostrophe before the *s* to show that the noun is functioning as a possessive adjective.

Mark It! Write ***adj*** above each adjective.

The mice feared the cat's (***adj***) claws.

Think About It!

Many words can be used as different parts of speech. However, a word can perform only one part of speech at a time.

Plural Noun: The maids stood in the kitchen.

In this sentence *maids* ends with an *s*. The *s* indicates that *maids* is a plural noun. There is more than one maid.

Possessive Adjective: The mice were scared of the maid's broom.

In this sentence *maid's* ends with an *apostrophe* + *s.* The *apostrophe* + *s* indicates that *maid's* is a possessive adjective. Whose broom? *maid's*

For more information about the possessive adjective, see page G-28.

Ask students to identify the possessive adjective.

Whose claws? ***cat's***
The apostrophe + s indicates that *cat's* is a possessive adjective, not a plural noun.

An apostrophe shows possession or indicates that letters are missing. These are the only reasons an apostrophe can be used.

Read It!	Mark It!	Fix It! Day 1
"during warm weather i like to work in the farmers garden," timmy **explained**	1 article (ar) 3 nouns (n) 1 pronoun (pr) 2 adjectives (adj) 2 prepositional phrases 2 subject-verb pairs (s v)	3 capitals 1 end mark 1 apostrophe

explained
made plain or clear

"during warm weather i like to work in the farmer's garden," timmy **explained.**

Capitalization	***During*** first word of the quoted sentence ***I*** personal pronoun I ***Timmy*** proper noun
End Marks	Use a period at the end of a statement.
Pronoun	***I*** replaces *Timmy*
Adjective	What kind of weather? ***warm*** Whose garden? ***farmer's***
S V Pairs	***I like***; ***Timmy explained*** *To work* is an infinitive. It does not function as a verb.

Rewrite It! "During warm weather I like to work in the farmer's garden," Timmy explained.

Read It!	Mark It!	Fix It!
johnny **considered** timmys reply. "what happens when it rains" johnny asked	3 nouns (n) 1 pronoun (pr) 1 adjective (adj) 1 adverb clause (AC) 4 subject-verb pairs (s v)	4 capitals 2 end marks 1 apostrophe

considered
thought carefully about

johnny **considered** timmy**'**s reply. "what happens **(**when it rains**)?**" johnny asked**.**

Capitalization	***Johnny*** proper noun; first word of the sentence ***Timmy's*** proper adjective ***What*** first word of the quoted sentence ***Johnny*** proper noun
End Marks	Use a question mark at the end of a question. Place it inside the closing quotation mark. Use a period at the end of a statement.
Pronoun	***it*** replaces weather
Adjective	Whose reply? ***Timmy's***
S V Pairs	***Johnny considered***; ***What happens***; ***it rains***; ***Johnny asked***

Rewrite It! Johnny considered Timmy's reply. "What happens when it rains?" Johnny asked.

Read It!	Mark It!	Fix It!
timmy explained that he stayed in his dry **burrow**, and ate corn and seeds when it rained	4 nouns (n) 2 pronouns (pr) 2 adjectives (adj) 2 coordinating conjunctions (cc) 1 prepositional phrase 1 *that* clause (that) 1 adverb clause (AC) 3 subject-verb pairs (s v)	1 capital 1 comma 1 end mark

burrow
a hole or tunnel in the ground where an animal lives

timmy explained (that he stayed in his dry **burrow**, and ate corn and seeds) (when it rained).

Capitalization	***Timmy*** proper noun; first word of the sentence
End Marks	Use a period at the end of a statement.
Pronoun	***he*** replaces *Timmy* ***it*** replaces weather
Adjective	What kind of burrow? ***dry*** Whose dry burrow? ***his*** The possessive pronoun *his* functions as an adjective.
S V Pairs	***Timmy explained***; ***he stayed***, ***ate***; ***it rained***
Commas	Do not use a comma to separate two items connected with a coordinating conjunction. **PATTERN a and b** *stayed* and *ate*

Rewrite It! Timmy explained that he stayed in his dry burrow and ate corn and seeds when it rained.

Read It!	Mark It!	Fix It!
he watched the red robin, which carefully hunted for **wriggly** worms	1 article (ar) 2 nouns (n) 1 pronoun (pr) 2 adjectives (adj) 1 -ly adverb (ly) 1 prepositional phrase 1 *who/which* clause (w/w) 2 subject-verb pairs (s v)	1 capital 1 end mark

wriggly
twisting; squirming

He watched the red robin, (which carefully hunted for **wriggly** worms).

Capitalization	***He*** first word of the sentence
End Marks	Use a period at the end of a statement.
Pronoun	***He*** replaces *Timmy*
Adjective	Which robin? ***red*** What kind of worms? ***wriggly***
-ly Adverb	Hunted how? ***carefully***
W/W Clause	***which carefully hunted for wriggly worms*** describes *robin*
S V Pairs	***He watched***; ***which hunted***

Rewrite It! He watched the red robin, which carefully hunted for wriggly worms.

Learn It!

Sentence openers are descriptive words, phrases, and clauses that are added to the beginning of a sentence. Using different sentence openers makes writing more interesting.

In this book you will learn three types of sentence openers—three ways to open or begin a sentence. After you mark a sentence, determine if the sentence begins with an opener that you know. If it does, mark it! Do not mark questions or quoted sentences.

There are six IEW sentence openers. This book will teach three of them.

#1 Subject Opener

A **#1 subject opener** is a sentence that begins with the subject of the sentence. Sometimes, an article or adjective will come before the subject, but the sentence is still a #1 subject opener.

For more information about the #1 subject opener, see page G-42.

Timmy jumped into the hole.

This sentence begins with the subject (Timmy). It is a #1 subject opener.

The three mice jumped into the hole.

This sentence has an article and adjective before the subject (mice). It is still a #1 subject opener.

Mark It! Write (1) above the first word of a sentence that starts with a subject opener.

(1) S V
Timmy crept into bed.

(1) S V V
Poor Timmy could not sleep.

After students mark the sentence, ask them to identify the opener.

The first sentence is a #1 subject opener because it begins with the subject of the sentence (Timmy).

The second sentence is a #1 subject opener because it begins with the subject of the sentence (Timmy). It has an adjective (Poor) in front of the subject but no other words.

Students will mark every subject opener unless it is a question or a quoted sentence.

Read It!	Mark It!	Fix It! Day 1
timmy was happier in the country because he **rarely** noticed loud, or sudden sounds their	1 article (ar) 3 nouns (n) 1 pronoun (pr) 3 adjectives (adj) 1 -ly adverb (ly) 1 coordinating conjunction (cc) 1 prepositional phrase 1 adverb clause (AC) 2 subject-verb pairs (s v) 1 opener	1 capital 1 comma 1 end mark 1 homophone

rarely
not often

(1) subject

timmy [s n] was [v] happier [adj] in the [ar] country [n] (because [AC] he [s pr] **rarely** [ly] noticed [v] loud [adj], or [cc] sudden [adj] sounds [n] ~~their~~ there).

Capitalization	***Timmy*** proper noun; first word of the sentence
End Marks	Use a period at the end of a statement.
Pronoun	***he*** replaces *Timmy*
Adjective	The adjective *happier* follows the linking verb and describes the subject (Timmy). What kind of Timmy? ***happier*** What kind of sounds? ***loud*** or ***sudden***
-ly Adverb	Noticed when? ***rarely***
S V Pairs	***Timmy was***; ***he noticed***
Commas	Do not use a comma to separate two items connected with a coordinating conjunction. **PATTERN a and b** *loud* or *sudden*
Homophones	Use ***there***, the adverb pointing to a place.

Rewrite It! Timmy was happier in the country because he rarely noticed loud or sudden sounds there.

Read It!	Mark It!	Fix It! Day 2
they suddenly heard the cats **troublesome** bell. johnny shouted, "yikes! you must follow me"	1 article (ar) 2 nouns (n) 3 pronouns (pr) 2 adjectives (adj) 1 -ly adverb (ly) 1 interjection (int) 3 subject-verb pairs (s v) 2 openers	4 capitals 1 end mark 1 apostrophe

troublesome
causing difficulty

(1) subject — s pr / ly / v / ar / adj / adj / n

they suddenly heard the cat**'**s **troublesome** bell.

(1) subject — s n / v / int / s pr / v / v / pr

johnny shouted, "yikes! you must follow me**!**"

Capitalization	***They*** first word of the sentence ***Johnny*** proper noun; first word of the sentence ***Yikes*** first word of the quoted sentence ***You*** first word following an interjection that uses an exclamation mark
End Marks	Use an exclamation mark at the end of a sentence that expresses strong emotion. Place it inside the closing quotation mark.
Pronoun	***They*** replaces *Johnny* and *Timmy* ***You*** replaces *Timmy* ***me*** replaces *Johnny*
Adjective	What kind of bell? ***troublesome*** Whose troublesome bell? ***cat's***
-ly Adverb	Heard when? ***suddenly***
S V Pairs	***They heard***; ***Johnny shouted***; ***You must follow***

Rewrite It! They suddenly heard the cat's troublesome bell. Johnny shouted, "Yikes! You must follow me!"

Read It!	Mark It!	Fix It!
the to mice fled to the dark cellar, which catnap usually **avoided**	2 articles (ar)	2 capitals
	3 nouns (n)	1 end mark
	2 adjectives (adj)	1 homophone
avoided stayed away from	1 -ly adverb (ly)	
	1 prepositional phrase	
	1 *who/which* clause (w/w)	
	2 subject-verb pairs (s v)	
	1 opener	

(1) subject

the ~~to~~ (two) mice fled to the dark cellar, (which catnap usually **avoided**).

Capitalization	***The*** first word of the sentence ***Catnap*** proper noun
End Marks	Use a period at the end of a statement.
Adjective	How many mice? ***two*** What kind of cellar? ***dark***
-ly Adverb	Avoided when? ***usually***
W/W Clause	***which Catnap usually avoided*** describes *cellar*
S V Pairs	***mice fled***; ***Catnap avoided***
Homophones	Use ***two***, the number.

Rewrite It! The two mice fled to the dark cellar, which Catnap usually avoided.

Read It!	Mark It!	Fix It!
johnny whispered from there hiding place, "im **disappointed** timmy. dont you want to stay with me"	3 nouns (n) 3 pronouns (pr) 3 adjectives (adj) 2 prepositional phrases 3 subject-verb pairs (s v) 1 opener	4 capitals 1 comma 1 end mark 1 homophone 2 apostrophes

disappointed
unhappy because what was hoped for did not happen

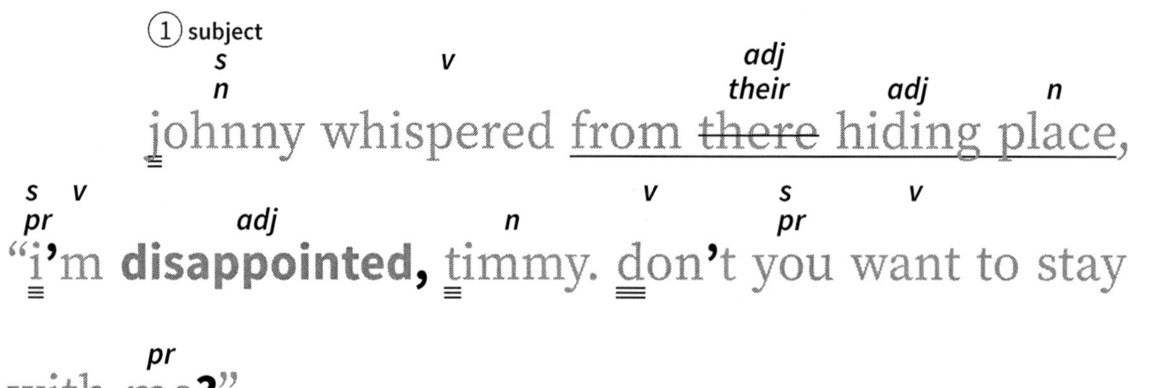

Capitalization	***Johnny*** proper noun; first word of the sentence ***I'm*** personal pronoun I; first word of the quoted sentence ***Timmy*** proper noun ***Don't*** first word of the quoted sentence
End Marks	Use a question mark at the end of a question. Place it inside the closing quotation mark.
Pronoun	***I***; ***me*** replace *Johnny* ***you*** replaces *Timmy*
Adjective	Which place? ***hiding*** A word that ends in -ing functions as a verb only if it follows a helping verb. Whose hiding place? ***their*** The possessive pronoun *their* functions as an adjective. The adjective *disappointed* follows the linking verb and describes the subject (I). What kind of I (Johnny)? ***disappointed***
S V Pairs	**Johnny whispered; I'm; you Do want** The contraction *I'm* includes both a subject (I) and a verb (am). The contraction *don't* includes both a helping verb (do) and an adverb (not). *To stay* is an infinitive. It does not function as a verb.
Commas	Place commas around a noun of direct address (NDA). ***, Timmy***
Homophones	Use ***their***, the possessive pronoun.

Rewrite It! Johnny whispered from their hiding place, "I'm disappointed, Timmy. Don't you want to stay with me?"

Learn It!

#2 Prepositional Opener

A **#2 prepositional opener** is a sentence that begins with a prepositional phrase. The first word in the sentence must be a preposition.

With great fear Timmy ran from the cat.

This sentence begins with a prepositional phrase (With great fear). It is a #2 prepositional opener.

Mark It! Write ② above the first word of a sentence that starts with a prepositional phrase.

②
In the kitchen the cook gave all the instructions.

②
In the large warm kitchen, the cook gave all the instructions.

②
During the sunny days in June, Timmy missed his garden.

If a prepositional opener has five words or more, follow it with a comma.

If two or more prepositional phrases open a sentence, follow the last phrase with a comma.

For more information about the #2 prepositional opener, see page G-42.

Pattern: preposition + noun (no verb)

After students mark the sentence, ask them to identify the opener.

Each sentence is a #2 prepositional opener because each begins with a prepositional phrase.

Students will mark every subject opener and prepositional opener unless it is a question or a quoted sentence.

A third comma rule states if a prepositional opener functions as a transition, follow it with a comma. In this book students do not need to determine if a prepositional phrase is a transition.

Require students to copy the commas correctly when they rewrite the passages.

Read It!	Mark It!	Fix It!
after a few minutes timmy, who didnt want to upset his new friend, **apologized**	1 article (ar) 3 nouns (n) 3 adjectives (adj) 1 prepositional phrase 1 *who/which* clause (w/w) 2 subject-verb pairs (s v) 1 opener	Day 1 2 capitals 1 end mark 1 apostrophe

apologized
showed sorrow for having insulted another

② prepositional

after a few minutes timmy, (who didn't want to upset his new friend), **apologized.**

(ar: a; adj: few; n: minutes; s n: timmy; s w/w: who; v: didn't; v: want; adj: his; adj: new; n: friend; v: apologized)

Capitalization	***After*** first word of the sentence ***Timmy*** proper noun
End Marks	Use a period at the end of a statement.
Adjective	How many minutes? ***few*** Which friend? ***new*** Whose new friend? ***his*** The possessive pronoun *his* functions as an adjective.
W/W Clause	***who didn't want to upset his new friend*** describes *Timmy*
S V Pairs	***Timmy apologized***; ***who did want*** The contraction *didn't* includes both a helping verb (did) and an adverb (not). *To upset* is an infinitive. It does not function as a verb.

Rewrite It! After a few minutes Timmy, who didn't want to upset his new friend, apologized.

Read It!	Mark It!	Fix It!
poor timmy was **miserable.** he didn't fit in, and badly missed his home	2 nouns (n)	3 capitals
	1 pronoun (pr)	1 comma
	3 adjectives (adj)	1 end mark
	1 -ly adverb (ly)	1 apostrophe
miserable very unhappy	1 coordinating conjunction (cc)	
	2 subject-verb pairs (s v)	
	2 openers	

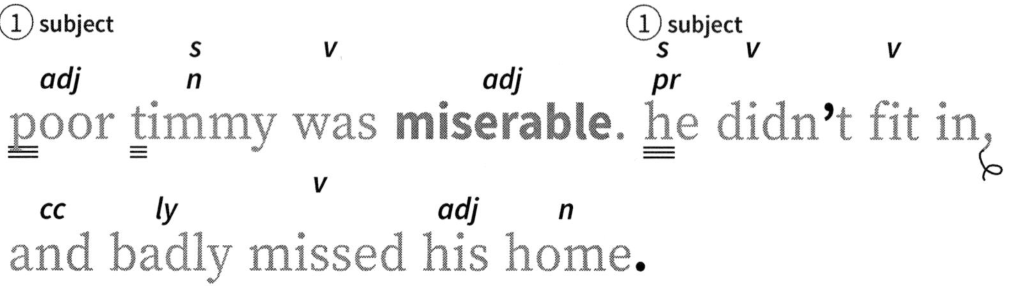

Capitalization	***Poor***; ***He*** first word of the sentence ***Timmy*** proper noun
End Marks	Use a period at the end of a statement.
Pronoun	***He*** replaces *Timmy*
Adjective	What kind of Timmy? ***Poor*** The adjective *miserable* follows the linking verb and describes the subject (Timmy). What kind of Timmy? ***miserable*** Whose home? ***his*** The possessive pronoun *his* functions as an adjective.
-ly Adverb	Missed how? ***badly***
S V Pairs	***Timmy was***; ***He did fit***, ***missed*** The contraction *didn't* includes both a helping verb (did) and an adverb (not).
Commas	Do not use a comma to separate two items connected with a coordinating conjunction. **PATTERN a and b** *did fit* and *missed*

Rewrite It! Poor Timmy was miserable. He didn't fit in and badly missed his home.

Read It!

after some thought johnny wisely **advised** timmy too return in the gardeners basket

advised
gave an opinion; suggested

Mark It!

1 article (ar)
4 nouns (n)
2 adjectives (adj)
1 -ly adverb (ly)
2 prepositional phrases
1 subject-verb pair (s v)
1 opener

Fix It!

3 capitals
1 end mark
1 homophone
1 apostrophe

(2) prepositional

after some thought johnny wisely **advised** timmy ~~too~~ to return in the gardener's basket.

Capitalization	***After*** first word of the sentence ***Johnny***; ***Timmy*** proper noun
End Marks	Use a period at the end of a statement.
Adjective	How much thought? ***some*** Whose basket? ***gardener's***
-ly Adverb	Advised how? ***wisely***
S V Pairs	***Johnny advised*** *To return* is an infinitive. It does not function as a verb.
Homophones	Use ***to***, the infinitive marker.

Rewrite It! After some thought Johnny wisely advised Timmy to return in the gardener's basket.

Read It!	Mark It!	Fix It! Day 4
until that moment timmy hadnt realized that he could go back. he joyfully **cried**, "can i leave soon"	2 nouns (n)	5 capitals
	3 pronouns (pr)	1 end mark
	1 adjective (adj)	1 apostrophe
	1 -ly adverb (ly)	
cried called loudly	1 prepositional phrase	
	1 *that* clause (that)	
	4 subject-verb pairs (s v)	
	2 openers	

(2) prepositional — adj, n, s n, v, v, that, s pr

until that moment timmy hadn**'**t realized **(**that he

(1) subject — v, v, s pr, ly, v, v, s pr, v

could go back**)**. he joyfully **cried**, "can i leave soon**?**"

Capitalization	***Until***; ***He*** first word of the sentence ***Timmy*** proper noun ***Can*** first word of the quoted sentence ***I*** personal pronoun I
End Marks	Use a question mark at the end of a question. Place it inside the closing quotation mark.
Pronoun	***he***; ***He***; ***I*** replace *Timmy*
Adjective	Which moment? ***that*** The first *that* functions as an adjective inside of a prepositional phrase. It does not begin a *that* clause because it is not followed by a subject and a verb.
-ly Adverb	Cried how? ***joyfully***
S V Pairs	***Timmy had realized***; ***he could go***; ***He cried***; ***I Can leave*** The contraction *hadn't* includes both a helping verb (had) and an adverb (not).

Rewrite It! Until that moment Timmy hadn't realized that he could go back. He joyfully cried, "Can I leave soon?"

Review It!

Verb

A **verb** shows action, links the subject to another word, or helps another verb.

An **action verb** shows action or ownership.

A **linking verb** links the subject to a noun or adjective.

A **helping verb** helps an action verb or a linking verb. The helping verb is always followed by another verb.

Answer these questions orally.

What must every verb have? a subject

The *be* verbs appear on both the linking verb and helping verb lists. What are they? am, is, are, was, were, be, being, been

Why is *could* a helping verb in the following sentence?

The cat could not catch the mice.

Could is a helping verb because it has another verb (catch) after it.

Add helping verbs to the action verb *missed* to change the meaning of the sentence. There are multiple right answers. Use *miss, missed,* or *missing.*

Timmy missed his home.

Timmy ______________________ his home.

The verb tense may change depending on the helping verb that is chosen. Possible answers include *will miss; had missed; could have missed; was missing.*

Find the weak verb and list possible stronger verbs. Have fun!

Timmy looked at the basket and longed for home.

____

Show students how to use a thesaurus.

Possible replacements for *looked* include *glanced, peered, stared.*

Read It!	Mark It!	Fix It!
johnny **sympathetically** told timmy that he could leave in the wicker basket on saturday if he was ready to leave	1 article (ar) 4 nouns (n) 2 pronouns (pr) 2 adjectives (adj) 1 -ly adverb (ly) 2 prepositional phrases 1 *that* clause (that) 1 adverb clause (AC) 3 subject-verb pairs (s v) 1 opener	3 capitals 1 end mark

sympathetically
with pity for someone else's misfortune

① subject

johnny **sympathetically** told timmy (that he could leave in the wicker basket on saturday) (if he was ready to leave).

Capitalization	***Johnny*** proper noun; first word of the sentence ***Timmy***; ***Saturday*** proper noun
End Marks	Use a period at the end of a statement.
Pronoun	***he***; ***he*** replace Timmy
Adjective	Which basket? ***wicker*** What kind of he (Timmy)? ***ready***
-ly Adverb	Told how? ***sympathetically***
S V Pairs	***Johnny told***; ***he could leave***; ***he was*** *To leave* is an infinitive. It does not function as a verb.

Rewrite It! Johnny sympathetically told Timmy that he could leave in the wicker basket on Saturday if he was ready to leave.

Read It!	Mark It!	Fix It!
since it was only tuesday, timmy had to wait **patiently** for saturday, which finally came	3 nouns (n) 1 pronoun (pr) 3 -ly adverbs (ly) 1 prepositional phrase 1 *who/which* clause (w/w) 1 adverb clause (AC) 3 subject-verb pairs (s v)	4 capitals 1 end mark

patiently
calmly; without irritation or complaint

(since it was only tuesday), timmy had to wait **patiently** for saturday, (which finally came).

Capitalization	***Since*** first word of the sentence ***Tuesday***; ***Timmy***; ***Saturday*** proper noun
End Marks	Use a period at the end of a statement.
Pronoun	***it*** replaces *Tuesday*
-ly Adverb	Was when? ***only*** Wait how? ***patiently*** Came when? ***finally***
W/W Clause	***which finally came*** describes *Saturday*
S V Pairs	***it was***; ***Timmy had***; ***which came*** *To wait* is an infinitive. It does not function as a verb.

Rewrite It! Since it was only Tuesday, Timmy had to wait patiently for Saturday, which finally came.

Read It!	Mark It!	Fix It!
on a **glorious** morning in june, timmy told the friendly town mice goodbye, and hid in the basket	3 articles (ar) 6 nouns (n) 3 adjectives (adj) 1 coordinating conjunction (cc) 3 prepositional phrases 1 subject-verb pair (s v) 1 opener	3 capitals 1 comma 1 end mark

glorious
delightful; brilliantly beautiful

(2) prepositional

on a **glorious** morning in june, timmy told the friendly town mice goodbye, and hid in the basket.

Capitalization	***On*** first word of the sentence ***June***; ***Timmy*** proper noun
End Marks	Use a period at the end of a statement.
Adjective	What kind of morning? ***glorious*** Which mice? ***town*** What kind of town mice? ***friendly***
S V Pairs	***Timmy told***, ***hid***
Commas	Do not use a comma to separate two items connected with a coordinating conjunction. **PATTERN a and b** *told* and *hid*

Rewrite It! On a glorious morning in June, Timmy told the friendly town mice goodbye and hid in the basket.

Read It!	Mark It!	Fix It!
as he left, timmy warmly invited johnny to the country for a **refreshing** visit	2 articles (ar) 4 nouns (n) 1 pronoun (pr) 1 adjective (adj) 1 -ly adverb (ly) 2 prepositional phrases 1 adverb clause (AC) 2 subject-verb pairs (s v)	3 capitals 1 end mark

refreshing
making one feel more rested and energetic

(as he left), timmy warmly invited johnny to the country for a **refreshing** visit.

Capitalization	***As*** first word of the sentence ***Timmy***; ***Johnny*** proper noun
End Marks	Use a period at the end of a statement.
Pronoun	***he*** replaces *Timmy*
Adjective	What kind of visit? ***refreshing***
-ly Adverb	Invited how? ***warmly***
S V Pairs	***he left***; ***Timmy invited***

Rewrite It! As he left, Timmy warmly invited Johnny to the country for a refreshing visit.

Learn It!

#3 -ly Adverb Opener

A **#3 -ly adverb opener** is a sentence that begins with an -ly adverb.

Foolishly, Timmy bit into a hot pepper.

This sentence begins with an -ly adverb (Foolishly).
It is a #3 -ly adverb opener.

Mark It! Write ③ above the first word of a sentence that starts with an -ly adverb.

③ *-ly*
Obviously, Timmy was hungry.

③ *-ly*
Eagerly Timmy ate a ripe cucumber.

Use a comma if an -ly adverb opener modifies the sentence.

Do not use a comma if an -ly adverb opener modifies the verb.

For more information about the #3 -ly adverb opener, see page G-43.

After students mark the sentence, ask them to identify the opener.

This sentence is a #3 -ly adverb opener because it begins with an -ly adverb (Obviously). *Obviously* is a sentence adverb. It modifies the entire sentence: it was obvious that Timmy was hungry. Use a comma.

This sentence is a #3 -ly adverb opener because it begins with an -ly adverb (Eagerly). *Eagerly* modifies the verb: Timmy ate in an eager manner. Do not use a comma.

In this book students do not determine if an -ly adverb modifies the sentence and needs a comma. However, discuss comma usage and require students to copy the commas correctly when they rewrite the passages.

Students will mark every sentence opener that they have learned unless it is a question or a quoted sentence.

Read It!	Mark It!	Fix It!
swiftly the cart **transported** the produce basket to timmys home in the country	3 articles (ar)	2 capitals
	4 nouns (n)	1 end mark
	2 adjectives (adj)	1 apostrophe
	1 -ly adverb (ly)	
transported moved from one place to another	2 prepositional phrases	
	1 subject-verb pair (s v)	
	1 opener	

(3) -ly adverb

swiftly (ly) the (ar) cart (s n) **transported** (v) the (ar) produce (adj) basket (n)

to timmy's (adj) home (n) in the (ar) country (n).

Capitalization	***Swiftly*** first word of the sentence ***Timmy's*** proper adjective
End Marks	Use a period at the end of a statement.
Adjective	What kind of basket? ***produce*** Whose home? ***Timmy's***
-ly Adverb	Transported how? ***Swiftly***
S V Pairs	***cart transported***

Rewrite It! Swiftly the cart transported the produce basket to Timmy's home in the country.

Read It!	Mark It!	Fix It! Day 2
cheerfully he walked through the **pleasant** garden, which looked beautiful too him	1 article (ar) 1 noun (n) 2 pronouns (pr) 2 adjectives (adj) 1 -ly adverb (ly) 2 prepositional phrases 1 *who/which* clause (w/w) 2 subject-verb pairs (s v) 1 opener	1 capital 1 end mark 1 homophone

pleasant
agreeable; enjoyable

③ -ly adverb

ly [c]heerfully s pr he v walked through ar the adj **pleasant** n garden,

w/w (which s v looked adj beautiful to ~~too~~ pr him).

Capitalization	***Cheerfully*** first word of the sentence
End Marks	Use a period at the end of a statement.
Pronoun	***he***; ***him*** replace Timmy
Adjective	What kind of garden? ***pleasant*** The adjective *beautiful* follows the linking verb and describes the subject (which). What kind of which (garden)? ***beautiful***
-ly Adverb	Walked how? ***Cheerfully***
W/W Clause	***which looked beautiful to him*** describes *garden* The relative pronoun *which* replaces the noun *garden*.
S V Pairs	***he walked***; ***which looked***
Homophones	Use ***to***, the preposition.

Rewrite It! Cheerfully he walked through the pleasant garden, which looked beautiful to him.

Read It!	Mark It!	Fix It! Day 3
on mondays he would **spot** the basket by the gate, but wouldnt get into it	2 articles (ar)	2 capitals
	3 nouns (n)	1 comma
	2 pronouns (pr)	1 end mark
	1 coordinating conjunction (cc)	1 apostrophe
spot	3 prepositional phrases	
find or recognize	1 subject-verb pair (s v)	
	1 opener	

(2) prepositional

on mondays he would **spot** the basket by the gate,
but wouldn't get into it.

Capitalization	***On*** first word of the sentence ***Mondays*** proper noun
End Marks	Use a period at the end of a statement.
Pronoun	***he*** replaces *Timmy* ***it*** replaces *basket*
S V Pairs	***he would spot*, *would get*** The contraction *wouldn't* includes both a helping verb (would) and an adverb (not).
Commas	Do not use a comma to separate two items connected with a coordinating conjunction. **PATTERN a and b** *would spot* but *would get*

Rewrite It! On Mondays he would spot the basket by the gate but wouldn't get into it.

Read It!	Mark It!	Fix It!
slowly the winter passed. in march the **brilliant** sun warmed the earth	3 articles (ar) 4 nouns (n) 1 adjective (adj) 1 -ly adverb (ly) 1 prepositional phrase 2 subject-verb pairs (s v) 2 openers	3 capitals 1 end mark

brilliant
shining brightly

(3) -ly adverb ... (2) prepositional

ly slowly · ar the · s n winter · v passed. · in · n march · ar the · adj **brilliant** · s n sun · v warmed · ar the · n earth**.**

slowly the winter passed. in march the **brilliant** sun warmed the earth**.**

Capitalization	***Slowly***; ***In*** first word of the sentence ***March*** proper noun
End Marks	Use a period at the end of a statement.
Adjective	What kind of sun? ***brilliant***
-ly Adverb	Passed how? ***Slowly***
S V Pairs	***winter passed***; ***sun warmed***

Rewrite It! Slowly the winter passed. In March the brilliant sun warmed the earth.

Review It!

Sentence Opener

A **sentence opener** is a descriptive word, phrase, or clause that is added to the beginning of a sentence. Using different types of sentence openers makes writing more interesting.

A **#1 subject opener** is a sentence that begins with the subject of the sentence.

Timmy climbed into the basket.

A **#2 prepositional opener** is a sentence that begins with a prepositional phrase.

In the morning Timmy climbed into the basket.

A **#3 -ly adverb opener** is a sentence that begins with an -ly adverb.

Finally, Timmy climbed into the basket.

Encourage students to practice forming sentences with different openers orally. Students who can easily create oral sentences struggle less when writing.

Practice writing sentences with different sentence openers.

Students may complete this exercise orally. There are numerous ways to form various sentence openers.

Write a sentence that begins with a #1 subject opener using the following words: mouse, arrived, garden.

A mouse arrived in the garden.

Add a #2 prepositional opener to your sentence.

By noon; With a basket; In the afternoon

Add a #3 -ly adverb opener to your sentence.

Eventually; Joyfully; Certainly

Rewrite the sentence with your favorite opener.
Add quality adjectives and -ly adverbs. Illustrate if you wish.

In the late afternoon a small, tired, hungry mouse eventually arrived in the lush, overgrown garden.

Read It!	Mark It!	Fix It! Day 1
shortly before noon 1 **dazzling** spring day, timmy sat by his burrow	4 nouns (n)	2 capitals
	4 adjectives (adj)	1 end mark
	1 -ly adverb (ly)	1 number
	2 prepositional phrases	
dazzling so bright it is blinding	1 subject-verb pair (s v)	
	1 opener	

(3) -ly adverb

shortly [ly] before noon [n] ~~1~~ one [adj] **dazzling** [adj] spring [adj] day [n], timmy [s n] sat [v] by his [adj] burrow [n].

Capitalization	***Shortly*** first word of the sentence ***Timmy*** proper noun
End Marks	Use a period at the end of a statement.
Adjective	Which day? ***spring*** What kind of spring day? ***dazzling*** How many dazzling spring days? ***one*** Whose burrow? ***his*** The possessive pronoun *his* functions as an adjective.
-ly Adverb	Sat when? ***Shortly (before noon)***
S V Pairs	***Timmy sat***

Rewrite It! Shortly before noon one dazzling spring day, Timmy sat by his burrow.

Read It!	Mark It!	Fix It!
happily he sniffed the bright, **fragrant** violets, and the newly cut grass. life was wonderful	2 articles (ar) 3 nouns (n) 1 pronoun (pr) 4 adjectives (adj) 2 -ly adverbs (ly) 1 coordinating conjunction (cc) 2 subject-verb pairs (s v) 2 openers	2 capitals 1 comma 1 end mark

fragrant
sweet-smelling

(3) -ly adverb

ly happily *s pr* he *v* sniffed *ar* the *adj* bright, *adj* **fragrant** *n* violets, *cc* and *ar* the

ly newly *adj* cut *n* grass. (1) subject *s n* life *v* was *adj* wonderful**.**

Capitalization	***Happily***; ***Life*** first word of the sentence
End Marks	Use a period at the end of a statement.
Pronoun	***he*** replaces *Timmy*
Adjective	What kind of violets? ***bright*** What kind of violets? ***fragrant*** What kind of grass? ***cut*** The adjective *wonderful* follows the linking verb and describes the subject (Life). What kind of life? ***wonderful***
-ly Adverb	Sniffed how? ***Happily*** Cut when? ***newly***
S V Pairs	***he sniffed***; ***Life was***
Commas	Do not use a comma to separate two items connected with a coordinating conjunction. **PATTERN a and b** *violets* and *grass*

Rewrite It! Happily he sniffed the bright, fragrant violets and the newly cut grass. Life was wonderful.

Read It!	Mark It!	Fix It!
he had **nearly** forgotten last years adventure, which had taken him to town by surprise	3 nouns (n)	1 capital
	2 pronouns (pr)	1 end mark
	2 adjectives (adj)	1 apostrophe
	1 -ly adverb (ly)	
nearly almost	2 prepositional phrases	
	1 *who/which* clause (w/w)	
	2 subject-verb pairs (s v)	
	1 opener	

① subject

s pr he v had ly **nearly** v forgotten adj last adj year's n adventure,

w/w (s which v had v taken pr him to n town by n surprise).

Capitalization	***He*** first word of the sentence
End Marks	Use a period at the end of a statement.
Pronoun	***He***; ***him*** replace *Timmy*
Adjective	Whose adventure? ***year's*** Which year's adventure? ***last***
-ly Adverb	Had forgotten to what extent? ***nearly***
W/W Clause	***which had taken him to town by surprise*** describes *adventure*
S V Pairs	***He had forgotten***; ***which had taken***

Rewrite It! He had nearly forgotten last year's adventure, which had taken him to town by surprise.

Read It!	Mark It!	Fix It!
as he **lazily** enjoyed his gardens beauty, someone suddenly appeared on the path. who was it	1 article (ar) 2 nouns (n) 2 pronouns (pr) 2 adjectives (adj) 2 -ly adverbs (ly) 1 prepositional phrase 1 adverb clause (AC) 3 subject-verb pairs (s v)	2 capitals 1 end mark 1 apostrophe

lazily
idly; without work or much effort

(as he **lazily** enjoyed his garden's beauty),

someone suddenly appeared on the path. who was it?

Capitalization	***As***; ***Who*** first word of the sentence
End Marks	Use a question mark at the end of a question.
Pronoun	***he*** replaces *Timmy* ***it*** replaces *someone*
Adjective	Whose beauty? ***garden's*** Whose garden's beauty? ***his*** The possessive pronoun *his* functions as an adjective.
-ly Adverb	Enjoyed how? ***lazily*** Appeared when? ***suddenly***
S V Pairs	***he enjoyed***; ***someone appeared***; ***Who was***
Note	In the second sentence *Who* does not start a *who/which* clause. *Who* begins a question.

Rewrite It! As he lazily enjoyed his garden's beauty, someone suddenly appeared on the path. Who was it?

Review It!

Strong Verb, Quality Adjective, and -ly Adverb

A strong verb, a quality adjective, and an -ly adverb are three different ways to dress up writing. These stylistic devices add a strong image and feeling.

A **strong verb** is an action verb, never a linking or helping verb.

A **quality adjective** is more specific than a weak adjective. A weak adjective is overused, boring, or vague.

An **-ly adverb** is used to enhance the meaning of the verb, adjective, or adverb that it modifies.

Find the weak verbs and list possible stronger verbs. Have fun!

Show students how to use a thesaurus.

Timmy went to town in a cart.

That evening the cat saw Timmy.

In his garden Timmy ate spring peas.

Consider how the verb changes the meaning of the sentence. For example, *Timmy devoured spring peas* evokes a different image than *Timmy nibbled spring peas.*

Add different -ly adverbs and quality adjectives to change the meaning of this sentence. There are multiple right answers.

Johnny __________ approached the __________ garden.

Johnny __________ approached the __________ garden.

Possible answers include *casually, slowly, eagerly; overgrown, humongous, lush.*

Continue to look for strong verbs, quality adjectives, and -ly adverbs in this book and write them on the collection pages found in Appendix II.

Read It!	Mark It!	Fix It!
it was johnny! he **strolled** into the garden with his walking stick leather bag felt hat and white gloves	1 article (ar) 6 nouns (n) 2 pronouns (pr) 5 adjectives (adj) 1 coordinating conjunction (cc) 2 prepositional phrases 2 subject-verb pairs (s v) 2 openers	3 capitals 3 commas 1 end mark

strolled
walked slowly in a pleasant and relaxed way

(1) subject (s pr) It (v) was (n) Johnny! (1) subject (s pr) He (v) **strolled** into (ar) the (n) garden with (adj) his (adj) walking (n) stick, (adj) leather (n) bag, (adj) felt (n) hat, (cc) and (adj) white (n) gloves.

Capitalization	***It***; ***He*** first word of the sentence ***Johnny*** proper noun
End Marks	Use a period at the end of a statement.
Pronoun	***It*** replaces *someone* ***He*** replaces *Johnny*
Adjective	What kind of stick? ***walking*** What kind of bag? ***leather*** What kind of hat? ***felt*** Which gloves? ***white*** Whose walking stick, leather bag, felt hat, and white gloves? ***his*** The possessive pronoun *his* functions as an adjective.
S V Pairs	***It was***; ***He strolled***
Commas	Use commas to separate three or more items in a series connected with a coordinating conjunction. **PATTERN a, b, and c** *stick*, *bag*, *hat*, and *gloves*

Rewrite It! It was Johnny! He strolled into the garden with his walking stick, leather bag, felt hat, and white gloves.

Read It!	Mark It!	Fix It!
without a pause timmy joyfully welcomed johnny, who looked **odd** in the garden	2 articles (ar) 4 nouns (n) 1 adjective (adj) 1 -ly adverb (ly) 2 prepositional phrases 1 *who/which* clause (w/w) 2 subject-verb pairs (s v) 1 opener	3 capitals 1 end mark

odd
different; unusual

② prepositional

without a pause timmy joyfully welcomed johnny, (who looked **odd** in the garden).

Capitalization	***Without*** first word of the sentence ***Timmy***; ***Johnny*** proper noun
End Marks	Use a period at the end of a statement.
Adjective	The adjective *odd* follows the linking verb and describes the subject (who). What kind of who (Johnny)? ***odd***
-ly Adverb	Welcomed how? ***joyfully***
W/W Clause	***who looked odd in the garden*** describes *Johnny* The relative pronoun *who* replaces the noun *Johnny*.
S V Pairs	***Timmy welcomed***; ***who looked***

Rewrite It! Without a pause Timmy joyfully welcomed Johnny, who looked odd in the garden.

Read It!	Mark It!	Fix It!
"your finally here johnny" **exclaimed** timmy as he shook johnnys hand	3 nouns (n) 2 pronouns (pr) 1 adjective (adj) 1 -ly adverb (ly) 1 adverb clause (AC) 3 subject-verb pairs (s v)	4 capitals 1 comma 2 end marks 1 homophone 1 apostrophe

exclaimed
cried out with strong emotion

"~~your~~ You're (s v, pr) finally (ly) here, johnny (n)!" **exclaimed** (v) timmy (s, n) (as (AC) he (s, pr) shook (v) johnny's (adj) hand (n)).

Capitalization	***You're*** first word of the quoted sentence ***Johnny***; ***Timmy*** proper noun ***Johnny's*** proper adjective
End Marks	Use an exclamation mark at the end of a sentence that expresses strong emotion. Place it inside the closing quotation mark. Use a period at the end of a statement.
Pronoun	***You*** replaces *Johnny* ***he*** replaces *Timmy*
Adjective	Whose hand? ***Johnny's***
-ly Adverb	Here when? ***finally***
S V Pairs	***You're***; ***Timmy exclaimed***; ***he shook*** The contraction *You're* includes both a subject (You) and a verb (are).
Commas	Place commas around a noun of direct address (NDA). ***, Johnny***
Homophones	Use ***you're***, the contraction for *you are*.

Rewrite It! "You're finally here, Johnny!" exclaimed Timmy as he shook Johnny's hand.

Read It!	Mark It!	Fix It! Day 4
timmy told him that they would **consume** there supper in the garden since it wasnt raining	1 article (ar)	1 capital
	3 nouns (n)	1 end mark
	3 pronouns (pr)	1 homophone
	1 adjective (adj)	1 apostrophe
consume eat	1 prepositional phrase	
	1 *that* clause (that)	
	1 adverb clause (AC)	
	3 subject-verb pairs (s v)	
	1 opener	

① subject

s n: timmy; v: told; pr: him; that: (that; s pr: they; v: would; v: **consume**; adj: ~~there~~ their

n: supper; ar: the; n: garden; AC; s pr: it; v: was; v: raining

Timmy told him (that they would **consume** ~~there~~ their supper in the garden) (since it wasn't raining).

Capitalization	***Timmy*** proper noun; first word of the sentence
End Marks	Use a period at the end of a statement.
Pronoun	***him*** replaces *Johnny* ***they*** replaces *Timmy and Johnny* ***it*** replace *weather*
Adjective	Whose supper? ***their*** The possessive pronoun *their* functions as an adjective.
S V Pairs	***Timmy told***; ***they would consume***; ***it was raining*** The contraction *wasn't* includes both a helping verb (was) and an adverb (not).
Homophones	Use ***their***, the possessive pronoun.

Rewrite It! Timmy told him that they would consume their supper in the garden since it wasn't raining.

Review It!

Coordinating Conjunction

A **coordinating conjunction** connects the same type of words, phrases, or clauses.

What are the seven coordinating conjunctions?

for, and, nor, but, or, yet, so

Students should follow the comma rules.

a and b

a, b, and c

Use some of the adjectives in the margin to write a sentence about the cat. Include a coordinating conjunction and punctuate correctly.

Adjectives to describe the cat

affectionate
cute
feisty
graceful
lazy
mellow
needy
playful

Find the coordinating conjunction and circle the words it connects.

The cook peeled the carrots, the onions, and the cucumber.

And connects three nouns.

The tired but alert mouse jumped out of the basket.

But connects two adjectives.

Should he run to the left or to the right?

Or connects two prepositional phrases.

Fill in the blanks with coordinating conjunctions. Some blanks have multiple right answers.

Catnap is a fast ___but___ unmotivated cat. For lunch he eats table scraps ___or___ goes without food. If he spies a mouse, he eagerly hunts ___yet___ rarely catches his prey.

Read It!	Mark It!	Fix It!
johnny loudly **complained** about the damp, and chilly weather. he wanted to go into the burrow	2 articles (ar) 3 nouns (n) 1 pronoun (pr) 2 adjectives (adj) 1 -ly adverb (ly) 1 coordinating conjunction (cc) 2 prepositional phrases 2 subject-verb pairs (s v) 2 openers	2 capitals 1 comma 1 end mark

Day 1

complained
found fault; expressed unhappiness

(1) subject
s v
n ly ar adj
johnny loudly **complained** about the damp,
(1) subject
s v
cc adj n pr ar n
and chilly weather. he wanted to go into the burrow.

Capitalization	***Johnny*** proper noun; first word of the sentence ***He*** first word of the sentence
End Marks	Use a period at the end of a statement.
Pronoun	***He*** replaces *Johnny*
Adjective	What kind of weather? ***damp*** and ***chilly***
-ly Adverb	Complained how? ***loudly***
S V Pairs	***Johnny complained***; ***He wanted*** *To go* is an infinitive. It does not function as a verb.
Commas	Do not use a comma to separate two items connected with a coordinating conjunction. **PATTERN a and b** *damp* and *chilly*

Rewrite It! Johnny loudly complained about the damp and chilly weather. He wanted to go into the burrow.

Read It!	Mark It!	Fix It!
suddenly a bee buzzed over johnnys head. he **ducked** in surprise. he was afraid	1 article (ar) 3 nouns (n) 2 pronouns (pr) 2 adjectives (adj) 1 -ly adverb (ly) 2 prepositional phrases 3 subject-verb pairs (s v) 3 openers	4 capitals 1 end mark 1 apostrophe

ducked
stooped or bent suddenly

③ -ly adverb

ly suddenly ar a s n bee v buzzed over adj johnny's n head.

① subject s pr he v **ducked** in n surprise. ① subject s pr he v was adj afraid.

Capitalization	***Suddenly***; ***He***; ***He*** first word of the sentence ***Johnny's*** proper adjective
End Marks	Use a period at the end of a statement.
Pronoun	***He***; ***He*** replace *Johnny*
Adjective	Whose head? ***Johnny's*** The adjective *afraid* follows the linking verb and describes the subject (He). What kind of he? ***afraid***
-ly Adverb	Buzzed when? ***suddenly***
S V Pairs	***bee buzzed***; ***He ducked***; ***He was***

Rewrite It! Suddenly a bee buzzed over Johnny's head. He ducked in surprise. He was afraid.

Read It!	Mark It!	Fix It!
johnny disliked the **unusual** smells sights and sounds of the country	2 articles (ar)	1 capital
	5 nouns (n)	2 commas
	1 adjective (adj)	1 end mark
	1 coordinating conjunction (cc)	
unusual	1 prepositional phrase	
not common or ordinary	1 subject-verb pair (s v)	
	1 opener	

① subject
s n johnny v disliked ar the adj **unusual** n smells, n sights, cc and

n sounds of ar the n country.

Capitalization	***Johnny*** proper noun; first word of the sentence
End Marks	Use a period at the end of a statement.
Adjective	What kind of smells, sights, and sounds? ***unusual***
S V Pairs	***Johnny disliked***
Commas	Use commas to separate three or more items in a series connected with a coordinating conjunction. **PATTERN a, b, and c** *smells*, *sights*, and *sounds*

Rewrite It! Johnny disliked the unusual smells, sights, and sounds of the country.

Read It!	Mark It!	Fix It!
after a moment johnny nervously asked timmy about the **monstrous** creature in the nearby field	3 articles (ar) 5 nouns (n) 2 adjectives (adj) 1 -ly adverb (ly) 3 prepositional phrases 1 subject-verb pair (s v) 1 opener	3 capitals 1 end mark

monstrous
extremely large and scary in appearance

② prepositional

after(ar) a moment(n) johnny(s n) nervously(ly) asked(v) timmy(n)

about the(ar) **monstrous**(adj) creature(n) in the(ar) nearby(adj) field(n).

Capitalization	***After*** first word of the sentence ***Johnny***; ***Timmy*** proper noun
End Marks	Use a period at the end of a statement.
Adjective	What kind of creature? ***monstrous*** Which field? ***nearby***
-ly Adverb	Asked how? ***nervously***
S V Pairs	***Johnny asked***

Rewrite It! After a moment Johnny nervously asked Timmy about the monstrous creature in the nearby field.

Review It!

Quotation Marks

Quotation marks indicate words are spoken.

Quote "Cows eat grass," **Attribution** the mouse explained.

The quote is the sentence in quotation marks. The attribution is the person speaking and the speaking verb.

Read the passage below. Underline the attribution and place quotation marks around the words that Johnny spoke.

When Johnny looked around the garden, he saw rows and rows of vegetables. He said, "I know that those green things are peas and those are beans. The bright red balls are tomatoes, of course. I am not sure what the long yellow vegetable is that is growing on the vine. What is it, Timmy?"

What would be a stronger verb than *said*? ____________________

Numerous words could replace *said*, including *observed*, *whispered*, *stated*.

Do you know what Timmy saw? ______________________________

Timmy saw a yellow squash.

Read It!	Mark It!	Fix It! Day 1
casually timmy told johnny not to worry. he explained, "its just a silly cow"	1 article (ar) 3 nouns (n) 2 pronouns (pr) 1 adjective (adj) 1 -ly adverb (ly) 3 subject-verb pairs (s v) 2 openers	5 capitals 1 end mark 1 homophone

casually
without serious thought

③ -ly adverb ... ① subject

ly casually; s n timmy; v told; n johnny; not to worry. s pr he

v explained, "s v pr It's ~~its~~ just a ar adj silly n cow."

casually timmy told johnny not to worry. he explained, "~~its~~ It's just a silly cow."

Capitalization	***Casually***; ***He*** first word of the sentence ***Timmy***; ***Johnny*** proper noun ***It's*** first word of the quoted sentence
End Marks	Use a period at the end of a statement. Place it inside the closing quotation mark.
Pronoun	***He*** replaces *Timmy* ***It*** replaces *cow*
Adjective	What kind of cow? ***silly***
-ly Adverb	Told how? ***Casually***
S V Pairs	***Timmy told***; ***He explained***; ***It's*** The contraction *It's* includes both a subject (It) and a verb (is). *To worry* is an infinitive. It does not function as a verb.
Homophones	Use ***It's***, the contraction for *it is*.

Rewrite It! Casually Timmy told Johnny not to worry. He explained, "It's just a silly cow."

Read It!	Mark It!	Fix It!
he added that johnny was **perfectly** safe if he avoided the cows feet, and the lawnmower	2 articles (ar) 3 nouns (n) 2 pronouns (pr) 2 adjectives (adj) 1 -ly adverb (ly) 1 coordinating conjunction (cc) 1 *that* clause (that) 1 adverb clause (AC) 3 subject-verb pairs (s v) 1 opener	2 capitals 1 comma 1 end mark 1 apostrophe

perfectly
completely; fully

① subject

he added (that johnny was **perfectly** safe) (if he avoided the cow's feet, and the lawnmower).

Capitalization	***He*** first word of the sentence ***Johnny*** proper noun
End Marks	Use a period at the end of a statement.
Pronoun	***He*** replaces *Timmy* ***he*** replaces *Johnny*
Adjective	The adjective *safe* follows the linking verb and describes the subject (Johnny). What kind of Johnny? ***safe*** Whose feet? ***cow's***
-ly Adverb	Safe how? ***perfectly***
S V Pairs	***He added***; ***Johnny was***; ***he avoided***
Commas	Do not use a comma to separate two items connected with a coordinating conjunction. **PATTERN a and b** *feet* and *lawnmower*

Rewrite It! He added that Johnny was perfectly safe if he avoided the cow's feet and the lawnmower.

Read It!	Mark It!	Fix It!	Day 3
in the garden timmy served a **peculiar** dish of purple eggplant with sprinkles of mint dill and parsley	2 articles (ar)	2 capitals	
	8 nouns (n)	2 commas	
	2 adjectives (adj)	1 end mark	
	1 coordinating conjunction (cc)		
	4 prepositional phrases		
	1 subject-verb pair (s v)		
	1 opener		

peculiar
strange; uncommon; unusual

(2) prepositional

in the garden timmy served a **peculiar** dish of purple eggplant with sprinkles of mint, dill, and parsley.

(ar: the, a; n: garden, timmy, dish, eggplant, sprinkles, mint, dill, parsley; s v: timmy served; adj: peculiar, purple; cc: and)

Capitalization	***In*** first word of the sentence ***Timmy*** proper noun
End Marks	Use a period at the end of a statement.
Adjective	What kind of dish? ***peculiar*** Which eggplant? ***purple***
S V Pairs	***Timmy served***
Commas	Use commas to separate three or more items in a series connected with a coordinating conjunction. **PATTERN a, b, and c** *mint*, *dill*, and *parsley*

Rewrite It! In the garden Timmy served a peculiar dish of purple eggplant with sprinkles of mint, dill, and parsley.

Read It!	Mark It!	Fix It!
johnny **suspiciously** poked at the odd vegetable while timmy asked him about his home, and family	1 article (ar)	2 capitals
	5 nouns (n)	1 comma
	1 pronoun (pr)	1 end mark
	2 adjectives (adj)	
suspiciously with distrust	1 -ly adverb (ly)	
	1 coordinating conjunction (cc)	
	2 prepositional phrases	
	1 adverb clause (AC)	
	2 subject-verb pairs (s v)	
	1 opener	

(1) subject

johnny **suspiciously** poked at the odd vegetable

(while timmy asked him about his home, and family).

Capitalization	***Johnny*** proper noun; first word of the sentence ***Timmy*** proper noun
End Marks	Use a period at the end of a statement.
Pronoun	***him*** replaces *Johnny*
Adjective	What kind of vegetable? ***odd*** Whose home and family? ***his*** The possessive pronoun *his* functions as an adjective.
-ly Adverb	Poked how? ***suspiciously***
S V Pairs	***Johnny poked***; ***Timmy asked***
Commas	Do not use a comma to separate two items connected with a coordinating conjunction. **PATTERN a and b** *home* and *family*

Rewrite It! Johnny suspiciously poked at the odd vegetable while Timmy asked him about his home and family.

Review It!

Sentence Opener

A **sentence opener** is a descriptive word, phrase, or clause that is added to the beginning of a sentence. Using different types of sentence openers makes writing more interesting.

Add prepositional phrase openers and -ly adverb openers to make these paragraphs more interesting to read. Use your own words or words in the margin.

By May the vegetables and fruit fill the garden. Bunnies visit the lettuce and cabbage heads. Occasionally chipmunks nibble on the corn, peas, and beans. Near the squash a goose has laid seven eggs. They will soon hatch, and the garden will be filled with baby birds.

In the middle of the garden is a scarecrow. Proudly he stands six feet in the air. Straw sticks out of his arms and legs. In the afternoon birds nap on his shoulders and sit on his head. Ordinarily mice like Johnny and Timmy scamper up his pant legs. Certainly the garden is a delightful place.

-ly adverbs

Certainly
Generally
Occasionally
Proudly
Surprisingly
Usually

prepositions

Beside...
By...
In...
Near...
With...

Read It!	Mark It!	Fix It!
johnny replied that they had problems, which **prompted** his visit to the country	1 article (ar) 4 nouns (n) 1 pronoun (pr) 1 adjective (adj) 1 prepositional phrase 1 *who/which* clause (w/w) 1 *that* clause (that) 3 subject-verb pairs (s v) 1 opener	1 capital 1 end mark

prompted
moved to action

① subject

johnny replied (that they had problems),
(which **prompted** his visit to the country).

Capitalization	***Johnny*** proper noun; first word of the sentence
End Marks	Use a period at the end of a statement.
Pronoun	***they*** replaces *family*
Adjective	Whose visit? ***his*** The possessive pronoun *his* functions as an adjective.
W/W Clause	***which prompted his visit to the country*** describes *problems*
S V Pairs	***Johnny replied***; ***they had***; ***which prompted***

Rewrite It! Johnny replied that they had problems, which prompted his visit to the country.

Read It!	Mark It!	Fix It! Day 2
he explained that the owners decided to **journey** too the seaside. they usually did this in the spring	3 articles (ar) 3 nouns (n) 2 pronouns (pr) 1 -ly adverb (ly) 2 prepositional phrases 1 *that* clause (that) 3 subject-verb pairs (s v) 2 openers	2 capitals 1 end mark 1 homophone

journey
travel

(1) subject
s pr he v explained (that that ar the s n owners v decided to **journey**

(1) subject
to ~~too~~ ar the n seaside). s pr they ly usually v did this in ar the n spring.

Capitalization	***He***; ***They*** first word of the sentence
End Marks	Use a period at the end of a statement.
Pronoun	***He*** replaces *Johnny* ***They*** replaces *owners*
-ly Adverb	Did when? ***usually***
S V Pairs	***He explained***; ***owners decided***; ***They did*** *To journey* is an infinitive. It does not function as a verb.
Homophones	Use ***to***, the preposition.

Rewrite It! He explained that the owners decided to journey to the seaside. They usually did this in the spring.

Read It!	Mark It!	Fix It! Day 3
before there trip the cook **declared** that she would remove the mice roaches and spiders from the house while they were at the seaside	4 articles (ar)	1 capital
	7 nouns (n)	2 commas
	2 pronouns (pr)	1 end mark
declared made known or stated clearly	1 adjective (adj)	1 homophone
	1 coordinating conjunction (cc)	
	3 prepositional phrases	
	1 *that* clause (that)	
	1 adverb clause (AC)	
	3 subject-verb pairs (s v)	
	1 opener	

(2) prepositional

adj their · *n* · *ar* · *s n* · *v* · *that* · *s pr* · *v*

before ~~there~~ trip the cook **declared** (that she would

v · *ar* · *n* · *n* · *cc* · *n* · *ar* · *n*

remove the mice, roaches, and spiders from the house)

AC · *s pr* · *v* · *ar* · *n*

(while they were at the seaside).

Capitalization	***Before*** first word of the sentence
End Marks	Use a period at the end of a statement.
Pronoun	***she*** replaces *cook* ***they*** replaces *owners*
Adjective	Whose trip? ***their*** The possessive pronoun *their* functions as an adjective.
S V Pairs	***cook declared***; ***she would remove***; ***they were***
Commas	Use commas to separate three or more items in a series connected with a coordinating conjunction. **PATTERN a, b, and c** *mice*, *roaches*, and *spiders*
Homophones	Use ***their***, the possessive pronoun.

Rewrite It! Before their trip the cook declared that she would remove the mice, roaches, and spiders from the house while they were at the seaside.

Read It!	Mark It!	Fix It! Day 4
unfortunately, she borrowed 4 kittens, and they're mother to help catnap	3 nouns (n)	2 capitals
	1 pronoun (pr)	1 comma
	2 adjectives (adj)	1 end mark
	1 -ly adverb (ly)	1 homophone
unfortunately unluckily; sadly	1 coordinating conjunction (cc)	1 number
	1 subject-verb pair (s v)	
	1 opener	

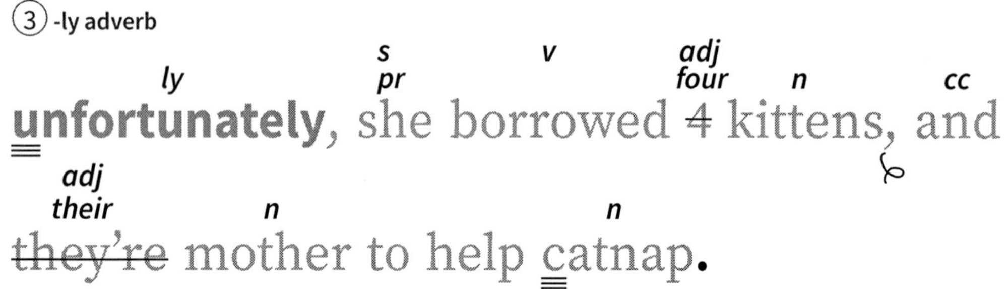

Capitalization	***Unfortunately*** first word of the sentence ***Catnap*** proper noun
End Marks	Use a period at the end of a statement.
Pronoun	***she*** replaces *cook*
Adjective	How many kittens? ***four*** Whose mother? ***their*** The possessive pronoun *their* functions as an adjective.
-ly Adverb	She borrowed four kittens how? ***Unfortunately*** *Unfortunately* is a sentence adverb. It modifies the entire sentence: it was unfortunate that she borrowed four kittens. For this reason, it doesn't answer a question about the verb but about the entire sentence. It requires a comma.
S V Pairs	***she borrowed*** *To help* is an infinitive. It does not function as a verb.
Commas	Do not use a comma to separate two items connected with a coordinating conjunction. **PATTERN a and b** *kittens* and *mother*
Homophones	Use ***their***, the possessive pronoun.

Rewrite It! Unfortunately, she borrowed four kittens and their mother to help Catnap.

Review It!

Adverb Clause

An **adverb clause** is a group of words that begins with a www word and contains a subject and a verb. An adverb clause must be added to a sentence that is already complete.

What is the adverb clause pattern? www word + subject + verb

What are the www words? when, while, where, as, since, if, although, because

Why is this an adverb clause? because the cat hissed
It contains a subject and verb: cat hissed.

Why is this not an adverb clause? because of the cat's hiss
This does not contain a subject and verb. This is a prepositional phrase.

Add adverb clauses to complete the paragraph.

The two mice decided to take a walk around the garden since ______________________________.

Although ______________________________, Johnny looked forward to the walk. The mice sang while ______________________________.

When ______________________________, the mice became scared. A horn honked and tires squealed because ______________________________.

Encourage students to practice forming complex sentences orally. Students who can easily create oral sentences struggle less when writing.

Each adverb clause must contain a subject and a verb. *Since morning* is not an adverb clause because it does not contain a subject and verb. *Since they wanted to exercise* is an adverb clause because it contains a subject (they) and a verb (wanted).

Read It!	Mark It!	Fix It! Day 1
timmy exclaimed, "5 cats are **horrendous**! your invited to stay through the spring and summer if youd like"	1 article (ar)	3 capitals
	4 nouns (n)	1 end mark
	2 pronouns (pr)	1 homophone
	2 adjectives (adj)	1 apostrophe
horrendous horrible; shockingly dreadful	1 coordinating conjunction (cc)	1 number
	1 prepositional phrase	
	1 adverb clause (AC)	
	4 subject-verb pairs (s v)	
	1 opener	

① subject

s n timmy v exclaimed, adj Five ~~"5~~ s n cats v are adj **horrendous**!

s v pr You're ~~your~~ v invited to stay through ar the n spring cc and n summer

AC (if s pr you'd v v like)."

Capitalization	***Timmy*** proper noun; first word of the sentence ***Five***; ***You're*** first word of the quoted sentence
End Marks	Use a period at the end of a statement. Place it inside the closing quotation mark.
Pronoun	***You***; ***you*** replace *Johnny*
Adjective	How many cats? ***Five*** The adjective *horrendous* follows the linking verb and describes the subject (cats). What kind of cats? ***horrendous***
S V Pairs	***Timmy exclaimed***; ***cats are***; ***You're invited***; ***you'd like*** The contraction *You're* includes both a subject (You) and a helping verb (are). The contraction *you'd* includes both a subject (you) and a helping verb (would). *To stay* is an infinitive. It does not function as a verb.
Homophones	Use ***You're***, the contraction for *you are*.

Rewrite It! Timmy exclaimed, "Five cats are horrendous! You're invited to stay through the spring and summer if you'd like."

Read It!	Mark It!	Fix It!
johnny replied that hed decide later. thunder rumbled in the distance as a huge raindrop **plopped** onto his nose	2 articles (ar)	2 capitals
	5 nouns (n)	1 end mark
	1 pronoun (pr)	1 apostrophe
plopped dropped or fell directly on something	2 adjectives (adj)	
	2 prepositional phrases	
	1 *that* clause (that)	
	1 adverb clause (AC)	
	4 subject-verb pairs (s v)	
	2 openers	

① subject (johnny: s, n) replied (v) (that he'd [that; he: s, pr] decide [v] later [v]). ① subject thunder (s, n) rumbled (v) in the (ar) distance (n) (as [AC] a [ar] huge [adj] raindrop [s, n] **plopped** [v] onto his [adj] nose [n]).

johnny replied (that he'd decide later). thunder rumbled in the distance (as a huge raindrop **plopped** onto his nose).

Capitalization	***Johnny***; ***Thunder*** first word of the sentence
End Marks	Use a period at the end of a statement.
Pronoun	***he*** replaces *Johnny*
Adjective	What kind of raindrop? ***huge*** Whose nose? ***his*** The possessive pronoun *his* functions as an adjective.
S V Pairs	***Johnny replied***; ***he'd decide***; ***Thunder rumbled***; ***raindrop plopped*** The contraction *he'd* includes both a subject (he) and a helping verb (would).

Rewrite It! Johnny replied that he'd decide later. Thunder rumbled in the distance as a huge raindrop plopped onto his nose.

Read It!	Mark It!	Fix It!
quickly the too mice **raced** into the toolshed. timmy grabbed a large sack, and a handful of leaves	4 articles (ar)	2 capitals
	6 nouns (n)	1 comma
	2 adjectives (adj)	1 end mark
	1 -ly adverb	1 homophone
raced ran quickly	1 coordinating conjunction (cc)	
	2 prepositional phrases	
	2 subject-verb pairs (s v)	
	2 openers	

Day 3

③ -ly adverb ... ① subject

ly quickly ar the adj two ~~too~~ s n mice v **raced** into ar the n toolshed. s n timmy

v grabbed ar a adj large n sack, cc and ar a n handful of n leaves.

Capitalization	***Quickly*** first word of the sentence ***Timmy*** proper noun; first word of the sentence
End Marks	Use a period at the end of a statement.
Adjective	How many mice? ***two*** What kind of sack? ***large***
-ly Adverb	Raced how? ***Quickly***
S V Pairs	***mice raced***; ***Timmy grabbed***
Commas	Do not use a comma to separate two items connected with a coordinating conjunction. **PATTERN a and b** *sack* and *handful*
Homophones	Use ***two***, the number.

Rewrite It! Quickly the two mice raced into the toolshed. Timmy grabbed a large sack and a handful of leaves.

Read It!	Mark It!	Fix It!
johnny asked, "timmy why are you **stuffing** that sack with dry leaves"	4 nouns (n) 1 pronoun (pr) 2 adjectives (adj) 1 prepositional phrase 2 subject-verb pairs (s v) 1 opener	2 capitals 1 comma 1 end mark

stuffing
filling by squeezing the contents into something

① subject

johnny asked, "timmy**,** why are you **stuffing** that sack with dry leaves**?**"

Capitalization	***Johnny*** proper noun; first word of the sentence ***Timmy*** proper noun; first word of the quoted sentence
End Marks	Use a question mark at the end of a question. Place it inside the closing quotation mark.
Pronoun	***you*** replaces *Timmy*
Adjective	Which sack? ***that*** The word *that* does not have to begin a clause. In this sentence *that* functions as an adjective. It does not begin a *that* clause because it is not followed by a subject and a verb. What kind of leaves? ***dry***
S V Pairs	***Johnny asked***; ***you are stuffing***
Commas	Place commas around a noun of direct address (NDA). ***Timmy,***

Rewrite It! Johnny asked, "Timmy, why are you stuffing that sack with dry leaves?"

Review It!

Contraction

A **contraction** combines two words into one. It uses an apostrophe to show where a letter or letters have been removed.

Form contractions with the following words.

it is it's

they are they're

was not wasn't

Match the words with the correct contractions.

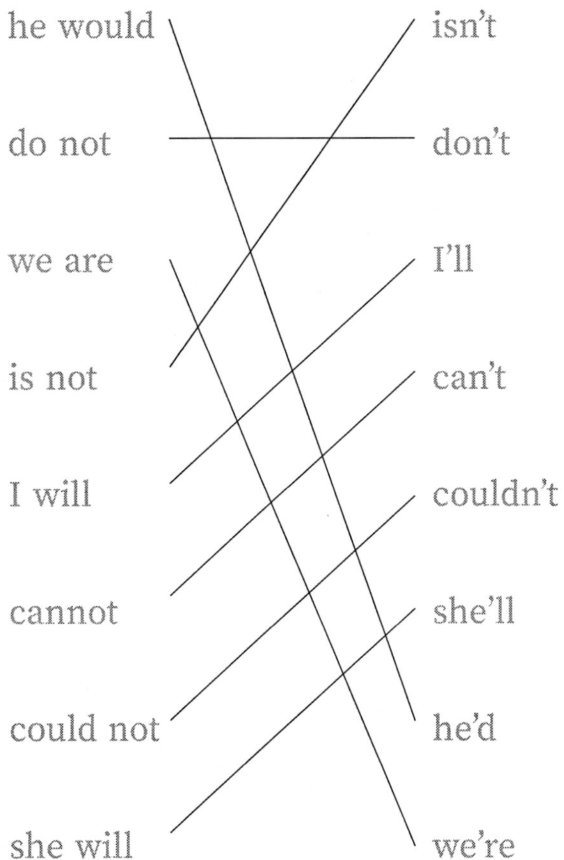

Read It!	Mark It!	Fix It! Day 1
timmy, who **busily** stuffed the sack, explained that it would be johnnys bed	1 article (ar)	2 capitals
	3 nouns (n)	1 end mark
	1 pronoun (pr)	1 apostrophe
	1 adjective (adj)	
busily full of activity or work	1 -ly adverb (ly)	
	1 *who/which* clause (w/w)	
	1 *that* clause (that)	
	3 subject-verb pairs (s v)	
	1 opener	

① subject

s n timmy, (s w/w who ly **busily** v stuffed ar the n sack),

v explained (that that s pr it v would v be adj johnny's n bed).

Capitalization	***TImmy*** proper noun; first word of the sentence ***Johnny's*** proper adjective
End Marks	Use a period at the end of a statement.
Pronoun	***it*** replaces *sack*
Adjective	Whose head? ***Johnny's***
-ly Adverb	Stuffed how? ***busily***
W/W Clause	***who busily stuffed the sack*** describes *Timmy*
S V Pairs	***Timmy explained***; ***who stuffed***; ***it would be***

Rewrite It! Timmy, who busily stuffed the sack, explained that it would be Johnny's bed.

Read It!	Mark It!	Fix It!
if hed known that johnny was coming, timmy would have **collected** freshly cut grass, and clover throughout the month of april	1 article (ar)	4 capitals
	6 nouns (n)	1 comma
	1 pronoun (pr)	1 end mark
collected gathered	1 adjective (adj)	1 apostrophe
	1 -ly adverb (ly)	
	1 coordinating conjunction (cc)	
	2 prepositional phrases	
	1 *that* clause (that)	
	1 adverb clause (AC)	
	3 subject-verb pairs (s v)	

(if he'd known) (that johnny was coming), timmy would have **collected** freshly cut grass, and clover throughout the month of april.

Capitalization	***If*** first word of the sentence ***Johnny***; ***Timmy***; ***April*** proper noun
End Marks	Use a period at the end of a statement.
Pronoun	***he*** replaces *Timmy*
Adjective	What kind of grass and clover? ***cut***
-ly Adverb	Cut when? ***freshly***
S V Pairs	***he'd known***; ***Johnny was coming***; ***Timmy would have collected*** The contraction *he'd* includes both a subject (he) and a helping verb (had).
Commas	Do not use a comma to separate two items connected with a coordinating conjunction. **PATTERN a and b** *grass* and *clover*

Rewrite It! If he'd known that Johnny was coming, Timmy would have collected freshly cut grass and clover throughout the month of April.

Read It!	Mark It!	Fix It! Day 3
during the night johnny **imagined** that unfriendly insects from the beds leaves were creepily crawling over him	2 articles (ar) 4 nouns (n) 1 pronoun (pr) 2 adjectives (adj) 1 -ly adverb (ly) 3 prepositional phrases 1 *that* clause (that) 2 subject-verb pairs (s v) 1 opener	2 capitals 1 end mark 1 apostrophe

imagined
thought; believed in his mind

(2) prepositional

s: johnny; v: imagined

ar: the; n: night; n: johnny; that: that

during the night johnny **imagined** **(**that

adj: unfriendly; s n: insects; ar: the; adj: bed's; n: leaves; v: were

unfriendly insects from the bed**'**s leaves were

ly: creepily; v: crawling; pr: him

creepily crawling over him**).**

Capitalization	***During*** first word of the sentence ***Johnny*** proper noun
End Marks	Use a period at the end of a statement.
Pronoun	***him*** replaces *Johnny*
Adjective	What kind of insects? ***unfriendly*** Whose leaves? ***bed's***
-ly Adverb	Crawling how? ***creepily***
S V Pairs	***Johnny imagined***; ***insects were crawling***

Rewrite It! During the night Johnny imagined that unfriendly insects from the bed's leaves were creepily crawling over him.

Read It!	Mark It!	Fix It!	Day 4
he wondered if anyone could **slumber** in a bed that hadnt been thoroughly washed, and cleaned	1 article (ar)	1 capital	
	1 noun (n)	1 comma	
	1 pronoun (pr)	1 end mark	
	1 -ly adverb (ly)	1 apostrophe	
slumber sleep	1 coordinating conjunction (cc)		
	1 prepositional phrase		
	1 *that* clause (that)		
	1 adverb clause (AC)		
	3 subject-verb pairs (s v)		
	1 opener		

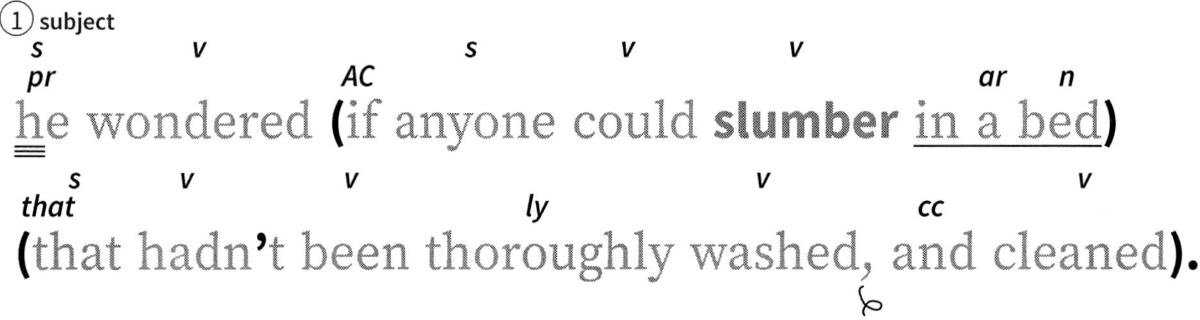

Capitalization	***He*** first word of the sentence
End Marks	Use a period at the end of a statement.
Pronoun	**He** replaces *Johnny*
S V Pairs	***He wondered***; ***anyone could slumber***; ***that had been washed***, ***cleaned*** The contraction *hadn't* includes both a helping verb (had) and an adverb (not).
Commas	Do not use a comma to separate two items connected with a coordinating conjunction. **PATTERN a and b** *washed* and *cleaned*

Rewrite It! He wondered if anyone could slumber in a bed that hadn't been thoroughly washed and cleaned.

9v26v24

Review It!

Adjectives and Adverbs

Both adjectives and adverbs add detail to a sentence. Adjectives tell more information about nouns and pronouns. Adverbs tell more information about verbs, adjectives, and other adverbs.

Adjective

- describes a noun or pronoun
- answers four questions: which one, what kind, how many, whose
- usually comes before the word it describes
- may follow a linking verb

Adverb

- modifies a verb, an adjective, or another adverb
- answers five questions: how, when, where, why, to what extent
- can come anywhere in a sentence
- often ends in -ly

Add adjectives and adverbs to complete the paragraph. Use your own words or words in the margin.

The ___little___ mouse that ___usually___ lives in the garden has ___gray___ fur. He has four ___teeny___ legs and a ___round___ belly. ___Surprisingly___ his ___thin___ tail is ___nearly___ as long as his body. He enjoys the ___lush___ garden because he ___regularly___ finds seeds, insects, and fruits in it. He ___commonly___ eats the most before the sun rises or after the sun sets.

adjectives
coarse
fat
gray
little
long
lush
round
small
tan
teeny
thin
vegetable

adverbs
astonishingly
commonly
consistently
continuously
frequently
nearly
periodically
rarely
regularly
routinely
surprisingly
usually

Read It!	Mark It!	Fix It!
over the next few days, the to mice explored the **enormous** garden as they gathered english peas cabbage leaves and carrots	3 articles (ar) 6 nouns (n) 1 pronoun (pr) 6 adjectives (adj) 1 coordinating conjunction (cc) 1 prepositional phrase 1 adverb clause (AC) 2 subject-verb pairs (s v) 1 opener	Day 1 2 capitals 2 commas 1 end mark 1 homophone

enormous
huge; immense

(2) prepositional

ar adj adj n ar adj two s n v

over the next few days, the ~~to~~ two mice explored

ar adj n AC s pr v adj n

the **enormous** garden (as they gathered english peas,

adj n cc n

cabbage leaves, and carrots).

Capitalization	***Over*** first word of the sentence ***English*** proper adjective
End Marks	Use a period at the end of a statement.
Pronoun	***they*** replaces *mice*
Adjective	How many days? ***few*** Which few days? ***next*** How many mice? ***two*** What kind of garden? ***enormous*** What kind of peas? ***English*** What kind of leaves? ***cabbage***
S V Pairs	***mice explored***; ***they gathered***
Commas	Use commas to separate three or more items in a series connected with a coordinating conjunction. PATTERN **a, b, and c** *peas*, *leaves*, and *carrots*
Homophones	Use ***two***, the number.

Rewrite It! Over the next few days, the two mice explored the enormous garden as they gathered English peas, cabbage leaves, and carrots.

Read It!	Mark It!	Fix It!
johnny **privately** thought that the country was to boring. nearly all of the food was plain vegetables	2 articles (ar) 4 nouns (n) 2 adjectives (adj) 2 -ly adverbs (ly) 1 prepositional phrase 1 *that* clause (that) 3 subject-verb pairs (s v) 2 openers	2 capitals 1 end mark 1 homophone

privately
secretly; not spoken publicly

① subject; s n: johnny; ly: **privately**; v: thought; (that: that; ar: the; s n: country; v: was; too (replacing ~~to~~); adj: boring). ③ -ly adverb; ly: nearly; s: all; prepositional phrase: of the food (ar: the; n: food); v: was; adj: plain; n: vegetables.

johnny **privately** thought (that the country was ~~to~~ too boring). nearly all of the food was plain vegetables.

Capitalization	***Johnny*** proper noun; first word of the sentence ***Nearly*** first word of the sentence
End Marks	Use a period at the end of a statement.
Adjective	The adjective *boring* follows the linking verb and describes the subject (country). What kind of country? ***boring*** What kind of vegetables? ***plain***
-ly Adverb	Thought how? ***privately*** To what extent was food plain? ***Nearly (all)***
S V Pairs	***Johnny thought***; ***country was***; ***all was*** The subject of a sentence is always a noun or a pronoun. The word *all* is an indefinite pronoun.
Homophones	Use ***too***, which means to an excessive degree in this sentence.

Rewrite It! Johnny privately thought that the country was too boring. Nearly all of the food was plain vegetables.

Read It!	Mark It!	Fix It!
hed give his shirt for some **savory** food like sausage pudding or steak	5 nouns (n)	1 capital
	1 pronoun (pr)	2 commas
	3 adjectives (adj)	1 end mark
	1 coordinating conjunction (cc)	1 apostrophe
savory pleasant in taste or smell	2 prepositional phrases	
	1 subject-verb pair (s v)	
	1 opener	

(1) subject

s/pr he'd (v) give (v) his (adj) shirt (n) for some (adj) **savory** (adj) food (n) like sausage (n), pudding (n), or (cc) steak (n).

Capitalization	***He'd*** first word of the sentence
End Marks	Use a period at the end of a statement.
Pronoun	***He*** replaces *Johnny*
Adjective	Whose shirt? ***his*** The possessive pronoun *his* functions as an adjective. What kind of food? ***savory*** How much savory food? ***some***
S V Pairs	***He'd give*** The contraction *He'd* includes both a subject (He) and a helping verb (would).
Commas	Use commas to separate three or more items in a series connected with a coordinating conjunction. **PATTERN a, b, and c** *sausage*, *pudding*, or *steak*

Rewrite It! He'd give his shirt for some savory food like sausage, pudding, or steak.

Read It!	Mark It!	Fix It!
it was **incredibly** quiet and dull their with nothing to do, and with nowhere to go	2 nouns (n) 1 pronoun (pr) 2 adjectives (adj) 1 -ly adverb 2 coordinating conjunctions (cc) 2 prepositional phrases 1 subject-verb pair (s v) 1 opener	1 capital 1 comma 1 end mark 1 homophone

incredibly
extremely

① subject

it was **incredibly** quiet and dull ~~their~~ there with nothing to do, and with nowhere to go.

Capitalization	***It*** first word of the sentence
End Marks	Use a period at the end of a statement.
Pronoun	***It*** replaces *country*
Adjective	The dual adjectives *quiet* and *dull* follow the linking verb and describes the subject (it). What kind of it (country)? ***quiet*** and ***dull***
-ly Adverb	Quiet and dull to what extent? ***incredibly***
S V Pairs	***It was*** *To do* and *to go* are infinitives. They do not function as verbs.
Commas	Do not use a comma to separate two items connected with a coordinating conjunction. **pattern a and b** *with nothing* and *with nowhere*
Homophones	Use ***there***, the adverb pointing to a place.

Rewrite It! It was incredibly quiet and dull there with nothing to do and with nowhere to go.

Review It!

Preposition

A **preposition** starts a phrase that shows the relationship between a noun or pronoun and another word in the sentence.

Complete the crossword puzzle by looking at the pictures below and choosing a preposition that explains the relationship between the mouse and the object in the picture.

Read It!	Mark It!	Fix It! Day 1
on sunday timmy was surprised to find johnny with his leather bag. johnny had neatly **arranged** his things in it	6 nouns (n) 1 pronoun (pr) 4 adjectives (adj) 1 -ly adverb (ly) 3 prepositional phrases 2 subject-verb pairs (s v) 2 openers	5 capitals 1 end mark

arranged
placed in a desired or proper order

(2) prepositional

on sunday timmy was surprised to find johnny with his leather bag. johnny had neatly **arranged** his things in it.

(1) subject

Capitalization	***On*** first word of the sentence ***Sunday***; ***Timmy***; ***Johnny*** proper noun ***Johnny*** proper noun; first word of the sentence
End Marks	Use a period at the end of a statement.
Pronoun	***it*** replaces *bag*
Adjective	The adjective *surprised* follows the linking verb and describes the subject (Timmy). What kind of Timmy? ***surprised*** What kind of bag? ***leather*** Whose leather bag? ***his*** The possessive pronoun *his* functions as an adjective. Whose things? ***his*** The possessive pronoun *his* functions as an adjective.
-ly Adverb	Arranged how? ***neatly***
S V Pairs	***Timmy was***; ***Johnny had arranged*** *To find* is an infinitive. It does not function as a verb.

Rewrite It! On Sunday Timmy was surprised to find Johnny with his leather bag. Johnny had neatly arranged his things in it.

Read It!	Mark It!	Fix It!
timmy realized that johnny **intended** to leave. he wanted johnny to stay in the country because it was calm, and safe **intended** planned or meant	1 article (ar) 4 nouns (n) 2 pronouns (pr) 2 adjectives (adj) 1 coordinating conjunction (cc) 1 prepositional phrase 1 *that* clause (that) 1 adverb clause (AC) 4 subject-verb pairs (s v) 2 openers	4 capitals 1 comma 1 end mark

(1) subject ... (1) subject

timmy [s n] realized [v] (that [that] johnny [s n] **intended** [v] to leave). he [s pr] wanted [v] johnny [n] to stay in the [ar] country [n] (because [AC] it [s pr] was [v] calm [adj], and [cc] safe [adj]).

Capitalization	***TImmy*** proper noun; first word of the sentence ***He*** first word of the sentence ***Johnny***; ***Johnny*** proper noun
End Marks	Use a period at the end of a statement.
Pronoun	***He*** replaces *Timmy* ***It*** replaces *country*
Adjective	The dual adjectives *calm* and *safe* follow the linking verb and describe the subject (it). What kind of it (country)? ***calm*** and ***safe***
S V Pairs	***Timmy realized***; ***Johnny intended***; ***He wanted***; ***it was*** *To leave* and *to stay* are infinitives. They do not function as verbs.
Commas	Do not use a comma to separate two items connected with a coordinating conjunction. **PATTERN a and b** *calm* and *safe*

Rewrite It! Timmy realized that Johnny intended to leave. He wanted Johnny to stay in the country because it was calm and safe.

Read It!	Mark It!	Fix It! Day 3
he argued that the town was **risky** because to many cats lived their	1 article (ar)	1 capital
	2 nouns (n)	1 end mark
	1 pronoun (pr)	2 homophones
	2 adjectives (adj)	
risky unsafe	1 *that* clause (that)	
	1 adverb clause (AC)	
	3 subject-verb pairs (s v)	
	1 opener	

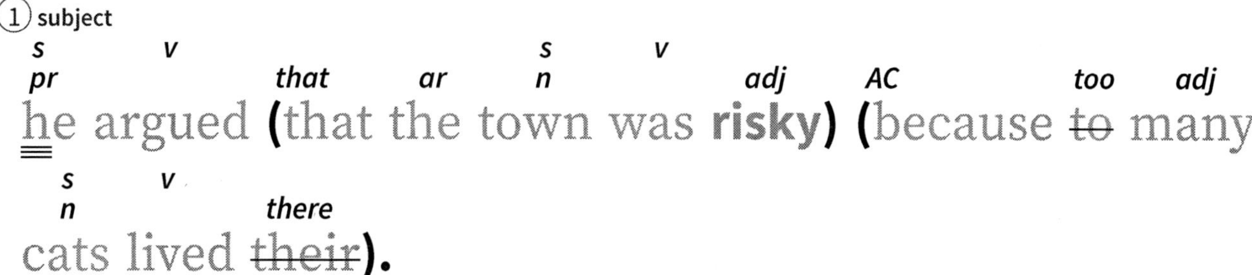

Capitalization	***He*** first word of the sentence
End Marks	Use a period at the end of a statement.
Pronoun	***He*** replaces *Timmy*
Adjective	The adjective *risky* follows the linking verb and describes the subject (town). What kind of town? ***risky*** How many cats? ***many***
S V Pairs	***He argued***; ***town was***; ***cats lived***
Homophones	Use ***too***, which means to an excessive degree in this sentence. Use ***there***, the adverb pointing to a place.

Rewrite It! He argued that the town was risky because too many cats lived there.

Read It!	Mark It!	Fix It! Day 4
johnny **protested**, "timmy you dont understand. town life is exciting because of the action the noise and the danger"	3 articles (ar) 6 nouns (n) 1 pronoun (pr) 2 adjectives (adj) 1 coordinating conjunction (cc) 1 prepositional phrase 3 subject-verb pairs (s v) 1 opener	3 capitals 3 commas 1 end mark 1 apostrophe

protested
argued

① subject

johnny **protested**, "timmy, you don't understand. town life is exciting because of the action, the noise, and the danger."

Capitalization	***Johnny*** proper noun; first word of the sentence ***Timmy*** proper noun; first word of the quoted sentence ***Town*** first word of the quoted sentence
End Marks	Use a period at the end of a statement. Place it inside the closing quotation mark.
Pronoun	***you*** replaces *Timmy*
Adjective	What kind of life? ***Town*** The adjective *exciting* follows the linking verb and describes the subject (life). What kind of life? ***exciting***
S V Pairs	***Johnny protested***; ***you do understand***; ***life is*** The contraction *don't* includes both a helping verb (do) and an adverb (not).
Commas	Place commas around a noun of direct address (NDA). ***Timmy,*** Use commas to separate three or more items in a series connected with a coordinating conjunction. **PATTERN a, b, and c** *action*, *noise*, and *danger*

Rewrite It! Johnny protested, "Timmy, you don't understand. Town life is exciting because of the action, the noise, and the danger."

10©1©24

Review It!

Fill in the blanks below with different parts of speech in order to create a silly version of "Town Mouse and Country Mouse."

After you have completed the list on this page, transfer your words to the blanks in the story on page 181.

2 adjectives ______________ ______________
1 -ly adverb ______________
2 nouns (food) ______________ ______________
1 adjective ______________
1 adjective ______________
1 verb (speaking verb) ______________
1 verb ______________
1 adjective ______________
1 verb ______________
1 adjective ______________
1 adjective ______________
1 adjective ______________
2 nouns (food) ______________ ______________
2 verbs (add -ing) ______________ ______________
2 nouns (animals) ______________ ______________
1 adjective ______________
1 verb ______________
1 verb ______________
1 verb ______________
2 nouns (food) ______________ ______________

Read It!	Mark It!	Fix It! Day 1
early on monday johnny **boldly** climbed into the basket, and arrived in town by the 1st day of may	2 articles (ar) 6 nouns (n) 1 adjective (adj) 2 -ly adverbs (ly) 1 coordinating conjunction (cc) 5 prepositional phrases 1 subject-verb pair (s v) 1 opener	4 capitals 1 comma 1 end mark 1 number

boldly
without fear

③ -ly adverb

ly early on n monday s n johnny ly **boldly** v climbed into ar the n basket, cc and v arrived in n town by ar the adj first ~~1st~~ n day of n may.

Capitalization	***Early*** first word of the sentence ***Monday***; ***Johnny***; ***May*** proper noun
End Marks	Use a period at the end of a statement.
Adjective	Which day? ***first***
-ly Adverb	Climbed when? ***Early*** Climbed how? ***boldly***
S V Pairs	***Johnny climbed***, ***arrived***
Commas	Do not use a comma to separate two items connected with a coordinating conjunction. **PATTERN a and b** *climbed* and *arrived*

Rewrite It! Early on Monday Johnny boldly climbed into the basket and arrived in town by the first day of May.

Read It!	Mark It!	Fix It!
this simple tale of to mice could be a true story, or a tall tale. in any case, it does **provide** a wonderful lesson	3 articles (ar) 6 nouns (n) 1 pronoun (pr) 7 adjectives (adj) 1 coordinating conjunction (cc) 2 prepositional phrases 2 subject-verb pairs (s v) 2 openers	2 capitals 1 comma 1 end mark 1 homophone

provide
supply or make available

① subject

adj adj s n adj two n v v ar adj
this simple tale of ~~to~~ mice could be a true

② prepositional

n cc ar adj n adj n s pr v v
story, or a tall tale. in any case, it does **provide**

ar adj n
a wonderful lesson.

Capitalization	***This***; ***In*** first word of the sentence
End Marks	Use a period at the end of a statement.
Pronoun	***it*** replaces *tale*
Adjective	What kind of tale? ***simple*** Which simple tale? ***this*** How many mice? ***two*** What kind of story? ***true*** What kind of tale? ***tall*** Which case? ***any*** What kind of lesson? ***wonderful***
S V Pairs	***tale could be***; ***it does provide***
Commas	Do not use a comma to separate two items connected with a coordinating conjunction. PATTERN **a and b** *story* or *tale*
Homophones	Use ***two***, the number.

Rewrite It! This simple tale of two mice could be a true story or a tall tale. In any case, it does provide a wonderful lesson.

Read It!	Mark It!	Fix It!
1 place **suits** 1 person while another place suits another person	4 nouns (n) 4 adjectives (adj) 1 adverb clause (AC) 2 subject-verb pairs (s v) 1 opener	1 capital 1 end mark 2 numbers

suits
fits; is appropriate for

(1) subject

adj One, s n, v, adj one, n, AC, adj, s n

~~1~~ place **suits** ~~1~~ person **(**while another place

v, adj, n

suits another person**).**

Capitalization	***One*** first word of the sentence
End Marks	Use a period at the end of a statement.
Adjective	How many places? ***One*** How many persons? ***one*** Which place? ***another*** Which person? ***another***
S V Pairs	***place suits***; ***place suits***

Rewrite It! One place suits one person while another place suits another person.

Read It!	Mark It!	Fix It! Day 4
truthfully, i **prefer** too live in the country like timmy. what do you prefer	1 article (ar)	4 capitals
	2 nouns (n)	1 end mark
	2 pronouns (pr)	1 homophone
	1 -ly adverb	
prefer like better	2 prepositional phrases	
	2 subject-verb pairs (s v)	
	1 opener	

③ -ly adverb

truthfully, i **prefer** ~~too~~ live in the country like timmy.

what do you prefer**?**

Capitalization	***Truthfully***; ***What*** first word of the sentence ***I*** personal pronoun I ***Timmy*** proper noun
End Marks	Use a question mark at the end of a question.
Pronoun	***I*** replaces narrator ***you*** replaces reader
-ly Adverb	I prefer to live in the country how? ***Truthfully*** *Truthfully* is a sentence adverb. It modifies the entire sentence: it was truthful that I prefer to live in the country. For this reason, it doesn't answer a question about the verb but about the entire sentence. It requires a comma.
S V Pairs	***I prefer***; ***you do prefer*** *To live* is an infinitive. It does not function as a verb.
Homophones	Use ***to***, the infinitive marker.

Rewrite It! Truthfully, I prefer to live in the country like Timmy. What do you prefer?

Word Game!

Use the words you chose on page 175 to complete the story.

Town Mouse and Country Mouse

by Leah
your name

Once upon a time a town mouse went on a visit to his cousin in the country. His cousin was ______ (adjective) yet ______ (adjective), but he made him ______ (-ly adverb) welcome. ______ (noun (food)) and ______ (noun (food)) were all he had to offer. However, the town mouse turned up his ______ (adjective) nose at this ______ (adjective) food. The town mouse ______ (speaking verb) his cousin that he needed to ______ (verb) to the town, and the ______ (adjective) mice ______ (verb) for the town.

When they had arrived, the ______ (adjective) town mouse took his cousin into the ______ (adjective) dining room. Soon the ______ (adjective) mice were eating up ______ (noun (food)) and ______ (noun (food)).

Suddenly they heard ______ (verb (add -ing)) and ______ (verb (add -ing)).

"What is that?" asked the country mouse.

"It is only the ______ (noun (animal)) or ______ (noun (animal)) of the house," answered the other.

Suddenly the door flew open and two ______ (adjective) dogs ______ (verb) in. The two mice had to ______ (verb) down and ______ (verb) off.

"I'm going home, Cousin," said the country mouse. "Better ______ (noun (food)) in peace than ______ (noun (food)) in fear."

Appendices

Town Mouse and Country Mouse

Johnny, the town mouse, was born in a kitchen cupboard filled with assorted tins of spices. Timmy, the country mouse, was born in a garden. It overflowed with vegetables. The two mice lived a long way from each other. An adventure brought them together.

It all started when Timmy traveled to town by mistake in a wicker basket. The basket belonged to a master gardener, who lived in northern England. What did he grow? He grew vegetables in his garden and fruit in his orchard. Each week he filled a basket with fresh produce. Then he set it by the gate. On certain days a carrier came. He took the wicker basket to town on a cart.

Early one Monday in April, Timmy snuck into the garden. The peas looked delicious! There he sat with his mouth stuffed full of spring peas. The large meal made him drowsy. Timmy stretched his paws and stifled a yawn. Where could he take a nap? Timmy noticed a basket beside the gate. He approached it without a sound. He crept into the basket and was soon asleep. It was perfect!

Timmy awoke abruptly in a fright, and the basket was lifted onto a cart. Suddenly the cart jolted, and the horse trotted to town. For two miles Timmy was tumbled around inside the basket.

Finally, the horse and cart stopped at a fancy house, which was located in a large town. The carrier, who was eager to finish his job, set the basket in the kitchen. Timmy heard the slam of the backdoor. He trembled with fear but was unharmed. Shortly after, the horse and cart rumbled away.

Inside the large house Sarah, the maid, noisily raced up the stairs and down the stairs too. The many noises terrified Timmy. He had lived his entire life in the peaceful and quiet country.

Soon Julia, the cook, opened and unpacked the basket, which contained prized vegetables. Suddenly Timmy jumped out of the basket. The tiny mouse surprised and dismayed Julia.

Julia jumped onto a sturdy chair and shouted, “Eek! It’s a mouse! Aah! I need help! Sarah, you fetch the long poker! Where is the cat?”

Naturally, Timmy did not wait for the long poker or the hungry cat, who was oddly named Catnap. Timmy fled along the baseboard and popped into a narrow hole at its edge. He dropped onto a wooden table. It was set for ten mice. The glasses, platters, and plates shattered.

"Who is this?" asked Johnny curiously. Johnny was an important town mouse.

"I am Timmy," squeaked the newcomer.

The unknown visitor had surprised Johnny, who quickly recalled his manners. With great politeness he introduced Timmy to nine other mice, who sat calmly with their lengthy tails, neckties, and jackets. In comparison, Timmy's vest, which he usually wore outdoors, was rumpled and dull.

Johnny kindly invited him to join them. They set an eleventh plate, cup, and napkin. The elegant feast included eight courses, which were served to the mice on one plate at a time. The city food was unfamiliar to Timmy, who normally avoided fancy dishes. He didn't want to join them, but he recognized that he'd seem terribly rude.

Sadly, the noise, which made Timmy jittery, didn't stop. He dropped a plate and a spoon. Johnny, who wanted to be a kind mouse, hastily said, "You don't need to worry. They aren't our plates."

Timmy saw that the two youngest mice had scurried upstairs. They returned with food for the table. For several minutes they gasped for breath. Timmy discovered that they had been chased by the cat, who was constantly looking for mice. Timmy squeaked shrilly. He feared that they would be hurt or killed. He was scared.

Johnny calmly said, "You've not eaten much food. Would you like cold milk and a biscuit with jelly?"

Timmy politely answered, "Johnny, I am too nervous to eat your food."

"Timmy, you're not eating. Maybe you should go to bed," Johnny quietly suggested.

They immediately went to a room upstairs. Johnny offered Timmy an ugly pillow, which looked comfortable. Timmy reluctantly sniffed the neat, clean, and unused pillow. Its wrinkly cover smelled like a cat. Timmy fearfully wondered if Catnap poked and prodded the pillow at night. Since he feared the cat, he had ghastly dreams about cats with teeth and claws.

When Timmy awoke in the morning, the town mice offered him a fancy breakfast. It smelled good. The mice, who enjoyed their food, proudly boasted that it was a dish with eggs in a cream sauce. Timmy couldn't easily digest their food because he needed fruit, nuts, and beans from his garden.

Throughout the day loud noises, which never stopped, disturbed Timmy. They seemed strange. Julia and Sarah pounded rugs in the afternoon while Catnap pestered the canary in its cage. During the evening the mice wandered through the house as they eagerly searched for tasty treats. At night Timmy couldn't sleep because of the tall clock, which noisily signaled each hour.

As time passed, Timmy longed to return to his quiet and peaceful home in the country. In late May Timmy confessed to Johnny that he wanted to leave because he missed his home, garden, and friends.

"You miss your garden? I would never miss fruits or vegetables," remarked Johnny. "What did you do there?"

"During warm weather I like to work in the farmer's garden," Timmy explained.

Johnny considered Timmy's reply. "What happens when it rains?" Johnny asked.

Timmy explained that he stayed in his dry burrow and ate corn and seeds when it rained. He watched the red robin, which carefully hunted for wriggly worms. Timmy was happier in the country because he rarely noticed loud or sudden sounds there.

They suddenly heard the cat's troublesome bell. Johnny shouted, "Yikes! You must follow me!"

The two mice fled to the dark cellar, which Catnap usually avoided.

Johnny whispered from their hiding place, "I'm disappointed, Timmy. Don't you want to stay with me?"

After a few minutes Timmy, who didn't want to upset his new friend, apologized. Poor Timmy was miserable. He didn't fit in and badly missed his home. After some thought Johnny wisely advised Timmy to return in the gardener's basket.

Until that moment Timmy hadn't realized that he could go back. He joyfully cried, "Can I leave soon?"

Johnny sympathetically told Timmy that he could leave in the wicker basket on Saturday if he was ready to leave. Since it was only Tuesday, Timmy had to wait patiently for Saturday, which finally came.

On a glorious morning in June, Timmy told the friendly town mice goodbye and hid in the basket. As he left, Timmy warmly invited Johnny to the country for a refreshing visit. Swiftly the cart transported the produce basket to Timmy's home in the country. Cheerfully he walked through the pleasant garden, which looked beautiful to him. On Mondays he would spot the basket by the gate but wouldn't get into it.

Slowly the winter passed. In March the brilliant sun warmed the earth. Shortly before noon one dazzling spring day, Timmy sat by his burrow. Happily he sniffed the bright, fragrant violets and the newly cut grass. Life was wonderful. He had nearly forgotten last year's adventure, which had taken him to town by surprise.

As he lazily enjoyed his garden's beauty, someone suddenly appeared on the path. Who was it? It was Johnny! He strolled into the garden with his walking stick, leather bag, felt hat, and white gloves.

Without a pause Timmy joyfully welcomed Johnny, who looked odd in the garden.

"You're finally here, Johnny!" exclaimed Timmy as he shook Johnny's hand.

Timmy told him that they would consume their supper in the garden since it wasn't raining.

Johnny loudly complained about the damp and chilly weather. He wanted to go into the burrow.

Suddenly a bee buzzed over Johnny's head. He ducked in surprise. He was afraid. Johnny disliked the unusual smells, sights, and sounds of the country.

After a moment Johnny nervously asked Timmy about the monstrous creature in the nearby field.

Casually Timmy told Johnny not to worry. He explained, "It's just a silly cow." He added that Johnny was perfectly safe if he avoided the cow's feet and the lawnmower.

In the garden Timmy served a peculiar dish of purple eggplant with sprinkles of mint, dill, and parsley. Johnny suspiciously poked at the odd vegetable while Timmy asked him about his home and family.

Johnny replied that they had problems, which prompted his visit to the country. He explained that the owners decided to journey to the seaside. They usually did this in the spring. Before their trip the cook declared that she would remove the mice, roaches, and spiders from the house while they were at the seaside. Unfortunately, she borrowed four kittens and their mother to help Catnap.

Timmy exclaimed, "Five cats are horrendous! You're invited to stay through the spring and summer if you'd like."

Johnny replied that he'd decide later. Thunder rumbled in the distance as a huge raindrop plopped onto his nose. Quickly the two mice raced into the toolshed. Timmy grabbed a large sack and a handful of leaves.

Johnny asked, "Timmy, why are you stuffing that sack with dry leaves?"

Timmy, who busily stuffed the sack, explained that it would be Johnny's bed. If he'd known that Johnny was coming, Timmy would have collected freshly cut grass and clover throughout the month of April.

During the night Johnny imagined that unfriendly insects from the bed's leaves were creepily crawling over him. He wondered if anyone could slumber in a bed that hadn't been thoroughly washed and cleaned.

Over the next few days, the two mice explored the enormous garden as they gathered English peas, cabbage leaves, and carrots.

Johnny privately thought that the country was too boring. Nearly all of the food was plain vegetables. He'd give his shirt for some savory food like sausage, pudding, or steak. It was incredibly quiet and dull there with nothing to do and with nowhere to go.

On Sunday Timmy was surprised to find Johnny with his leather bag. Johnny had neatly arranged his things in it. Timmy realized that Johnny intended to leave. He wanted Johnny to stay in the country because it was calm and safe. He argued that the town was risky because too many cats lived there.

Johnny protested, "Timmy, you don't understand. Town life is exciting because of the action, the noise, and the danger."

Early on Monday Johnny boldly climbed into the basket and arrived in town by the first day of May.

This simple tale of two mice could be a true story or a tall tale. In any case, it does provide a wonderful lesson. One place suits one person while another place suits another person. Truthfully, I prefer to live in the country like Timmy. What do you prefer?

-ly Adverb

An **-ly adverb** dresses up writing when it creates a strong image or feeling.

Strong Verb

A **strong verb** dresses up writing because it creates a strong image or feeling. A strong verb is an action verb, never a linking or helping verb.

Quality Adjective

A **quality adjective** dresses up writing because it creates a strong image or feeling. A quality adjective is more specific than a weak adjective, which is overused, boring, or vague.

Fix It!™ Grammar

Glossary

Fix It! Grammar

Glossary

FOURTH EDITION

Fourth Edition version 2, January 2022

Contents

Parts of Speech

Every word belongs to a word group—a **part of speech**. There are eight parts of speech. Many words can be used as different parts of speech. However, a word will only perform one part of speech at a time. (*Light* is a verb in The fireworks *light* the sky. *Light* is a noun in We need more *light*. *Light* is an adjective in It is a *light* load.)

One must look at how words are used in a sentence to determine their parts of speech. To see how these parts of speech are used as IEW dress-ups and sentence openers, see the Stylistic Techniques section beginning on page G-37.

Noun

A **noun** names a person, place, thing, or idea.

To determine if a word is a noun, ask if an article adjective (a, an, the) comes before it or if it is countable.

Noun Tests:
the ______
two ______

A **common noun** names a general person, place, or thing. It is not capitalized.

A **proper noun** names a specific person, place, or thing. It is capitalized.

The *king* is a common noun, but *King James* is a proper noun.

A *beagle* is a common noun, but the name of my pet beagle *Benji* is a proper noun.

A **compound noun** is two or more words combined to form a single noun. They can be written three different ways. To spell compound words correctly, consult a dictionary.

separate words	*fairy tale; Robin Hood; ice cream*
hyphenated words	*merry-go-round; son-in-law; seventy-two*
one word	*grandmother; railroad; moonlight*

Pronoun

A **pronoun** replaces a noun in order to avoid repetition. The noun the pronoun replaces is called an antecedent.

A **personal pronoun** refers back to an antecedent recently mentioned and takes the place of that noun. The pronoun should agree with its antecedent in number, person, and case.

	3 cases	*Subjective* function as	*Objective* function as	*Possessive* function as	
		subject subject complement	object of a preposition direct object indirect object	adjective	pronoun
2 numbers	3 persons				
singular	*1st*	I	me	my	mine
	2nd	you	you	your	yours
	3rd	he, she, it	him, her, it	his, her, its	his, hers, its
plural	*1st*	we	us	our	ours
	2nd	you	you	your	yours
	3rd	they	them	their	theirs

Number means one (singular) or more than one (plural).

Person means who is speaking (1st), spoken to (2nd), or spoken about (3rd).

Case refers to the way a pronoun functions in a sentence.

Both a **reflexive pronoun** (used in the objective case) and an **intensive pronoun** (used as an appositive) end in *-self* or *-selves* and refer back to a noun or pronoun in the same sentence.

Dorinda fancied *herself* quite stylish. Dorinda *herself* played as others worked.

A **relative pronoun** (*who, which, that*) begins a dependent clause. Use *who* for people and *which* or *that* for things. See page G-21.

Robin lived in Sherwood Forest, *which* belonged to the king.

Robin knew the other men *who* lived in the forest.

Robin battled with Little John, *whom* he had met on the log.

Robin knew the families *whose* lands had been stolen.

Forms of *who* include *whom* and *whose.*

who subjective case
whom objective case
whose possessive case

An **interrogative pronoun** is used to ask a question. The most common include *what, whatever, which, whichever, who, whoever, whom, whose.*

Who owns that house? *Whatever* do you mean? *Whose* coat is this?

Not all question words are pronouns. Words like *why* and *how* are adverbs.

A **demonstrative pronoun** (*this, that, these, those*) points to a particular person or thing.

This is my mother and *that* is our house. *These* are mine. *Those* are yours.

An **indefinite pronoun** is not definite. It does not refer to any particular person or thing.

Everyone will attend. *All* of the cookies are gone. *Most* of the cake is gone.

Singular and Plural	**Plural**	**Singular**			
all	both		each	much	one
any	few	another	either	neither	other
more	many	anybody	everybody	nobody	somebody
most	others	anyone	everyone	no one	someone
none	own	anything	everything	nothing	something
some	several	anywhere	everywhere	nowhere	somewhere

When a word on the demonstrative or indefinite list is placed before a noun, it functions as an adjective, not a pronoun.

Both cookies are gone.

I live in *that* house.

Noun and Pronoun Functions

Both nouns and pronouns perform many jobs or functions in a sentence.

A **subject** performs a verb action. It tells who or what the clause is about.

The soldier marched in formation.
Who marched? *soldier* (subject)

A **subject complement** follows a linking verb and renames the subject (also called a predicate noun) or describes the subject (also called a predicate adjective).

The soldier is a *woman*. The king is *he*. The castle is *theirs*.

The **object of a preposition** is the last word in a prepositional phrase. See page G-18.

A **direct object** follows an action verb and answers the question *what* or *whom*.

The soldier built a fire.
Built what? *a fire* (direct object)

The soldier treated him kindly.
Treated whom? *him* (direct object)

An **indirect object** appears only when there is a direct object. Indirect objects come between the verb and direct object and tell who or what received the direct object.

The dwarf gave the soldier a purse.
Gave what? *purse* (direct object). Who received it? *soldier* (indirect object)

The woman knitted him a scarf.
Knitted what? *scarf* (direct object). Who received it? *him* (indirect object)

To tell the difference between an indirect object and a direct object, revise the sentence and insert *to* or *for* in front of the indirect object.

The dwarf gave a purse *to* the soldier.

The woman knitted a scarf *for* him.

A **possessive case pronoun** that functions as an adjective comes before a noun, whereas a possessive case pronoun that functions as a pronoun is used alone.

That is *my* house.

That is *mine*.

A **noun of direct address** (NDA) is a noun used to refer to someone directly. It appears in dialogue and names the person spoken to.

"Timmy, after dinner we can read books," Johnny said.

An **appositive** is a noun that renames the noun that comes before it.

Place commas around an appositive if it is nonessential to the meaning of the sentence.

Robin Hood**,** *the archer***,** led his men through the forest.
(nonessential, commas)

Do not place commas around an appositive if it is essential to the meaning of the sentence. See page G-26.

The archer *Robin Hood* led his men through the forest.
(essential, no commas) The appositive is essential because it defines which archer led his men.

Function is different from part of speech.

A noun or pronoun can perform only one function in a sentence.

When the sentence is a command, the subject, *you*, is implied. See imperative mood, page G-11.

The appositive is an invisible *who/which* clause. See page G-39.

Preposition

A **preposition** starts a phrase that shows the relationship between a noun or pronoun and another word in the sentence.

PATTERN

preposition + noun (no verb)

A preposition usually shows a relationship dealing with space or time.

The squirrel sat *on the branch* (space) *in the morning* (time).

A word functions as a preposition when it is part of a prepositional phrase. See page G-18.

A prepositional phrase always begins with a preposition and ends with a noun or pronoun. The phrase may have adjectives in between, but never a verb.

The noun or pronoun that ends the prepositional phrase is called the object of the preposition. When the object of the preposition is a pronoun, it will be one of the objective case pronouns: *me, you, him, her, it, us, you, them.*

Some words on the preposition list may function as another part of speech.

When a word that looks like a preposition follows a verb but does not have a noun afterward, it is not functioning as a preposition but as an adverb.

The mouse fell down. (fell where? *down*)
Down is not followed by a noun.
This is an adverb, not a prepositional phrase.

Timmy wore his vest inside (wore vest where? *inside*)
Inside is not followed by a noun.
This is an adverb, not a prepositional phrase.

When a word that looks like a preposition is followed by a subject and a verb, it is a not functioning as a preposition but as a subordinating conjunction (www word).

As Johnny gave orders, the mice listened
As Johnny gave orders contains a subject (Johnny) and a verb (gave).
This is a clause, not a prepositional phrase.

The mice hid *after the cat arrived.*
After the cat arrived contains a subject (cat) and a verb (arrived).
This is a clause, not a prepositional phrase.

If it is something a squirrel can do with a tree, it is probably a prepositional phrase.

A squirrel
climbs *up the tree,*
sits *in the tree,*
runs *around the tree.*

This is not an exhaustive list. When in doubt, consult a dictionary.

Prepositions List

aboard	around	between	in	opposite	toward
about	as	beyond	inside	out	under
above	at	by	instead of	outside	underneath
according to	because of	concerning	into	over	unlike
across	before	despite	like	past	until
after	behind	down	minus	regarding	unto
against	below	during	near	since	up, upon
along	beneath	except	of	through	with
amid	beside	for	off	throughout	within
among	besides	from	on, onto	to	without

Verb

A **verb** shows action, links the subject to another word, or helps another verb.

To determine if a word is a verb, use the verb test.

Verb Test:
I _______.
It _______.

An **action verb** shows action or ownership.

She *chopped* vegetables.

The chef *prepared* lunch.

Dorinda *has* a beauty mark.

They *own* a lovely palace.

A **linking verb** links the subject to a noun or an adjective. When the subject complement is a noun, the noun after the linking verb renames the subject. When the subject complement is an adjective, the adjective after the linking verb describes the subject.

Robin Hood *was* (linking verb) an outlaw (subject complement, noun).
Outlaw is another name for Robin Hood.

The soup *smelled* (linking verb) delicious (subject complement, adjective).
Delicious describes soup.

The soup *is* (linking verb) salty (subject complement, adjective).
Salty describes soup.

Some verbs function as either action or linking verbs.

He *smells* (action) gas.

The gas *smells* (linking) bad.

If you can substitute *is* for the verb, it is probably functioning as a linking verb.

A **helping verb** helps an action verb or a linking verb. It is paired with the main verb (action or linking) to indicate tense, voice, and mood.

The chef *would* prepare supper.
Would helps prepare.

The soup *had* tasted strange.
Had helps tasted.

Linking Verbs List

am, is, are, was, were, be, being, been (be verbs)

seem, become, appear, grow, remain

taste, sound, smell, feel, look (verbs dealing with the senses)

Helping Verbs List

am, is, are, was, were, be, being, been (be verbs)

have, has, had, do, does, did, may, might, must

can, will, shall, could, would, should

Be verbs dominate our language and perform important functions as both linking and helping verbs.

Students should memorize the *be* verbs: am, is, are, was, were, be, being, been.

Verbal

A **verbal** is a word formed from a verb that is usually not functioning as a verb. A verbal often functions as a noun, adjective, or adverb.

An **infinitive** is formed by placing *to* in front of the simple present form of a verb.

An infinitive functions as an adjective, adverb, or noun, but never as a verb.

Dorinda has some things *to learn.*

Frederick is eager *to hear* a story.

A **participle** is formed by adding the suffix *-ing* or *-ed* to the simple present form of a verb.

splash + ing = splashing; splash + ed = splashed

A participle functions as a verb if it has a helping verb.

He *was splashing,* which frightened the fish.

For years, she *had longed* to visit the city.

If a participle does not have a helping verb, it functions as an adjective. A participle-adjective may appear directly before a noun or after a linking verb.

Robin Hood was known for his *hunting* skills.

It was a *botched* case. The case was *botched.*

A participle may also form a participial phrase that describes a noun in the sentence.

Springing to his feet, Robin Hood confronted the challenger.
Springing to his feet describes Robin Hood, the subject after the comma.

Robin Hood whistled merrily, *thinking of Maid Marian.*
Thinking of Maid Marian describes Robin Hood, the subject of the sentence.

A **gerund** is formed by adding the suffix *-ing* to the simple present form of a verb.

splash + ing = splashing

A gerund functions as a noun, never as a verb.

His *splashing* frightened the fish.
Splashing is the subject of the sentence and therefore a noun.

The fish were frightened by his *splashing.*
Splashing is the object of the preposition *by* and therefore a noun.

To + verb and verbs ending in -ing should not be marked as strong verbs.

For clarity in meaning, avoid splitting infinitives when possible.

To split an infinitive is to insert one or more adverbs between *to* and the verb, as in *to foolishly insert.*

Some words do not form the past participle by adding -ed. There are many irregular verb forms.

eat/eaten
not eated

creep/crept
not creeped

draw/drew
not drawed

If in doubt, consult a dictionary.

Tense

Verb tense indicates when an action occurs. There are six tenses in English: simple past, simple present, simple future, past perfect, present perfect, and future perfect.

The **simple tense** is simply formed by using different forms of the verb.

I *biked.* I *bike.* I *will bike.*

He *ran.* He *runs.* He *will run.*

The **perfect tense** is formed by adding a form of *have* to the past participle verb form.

I *had biked.* I *have biked.* I *will have biked.*

He *had run.* He *has run.* He *will have run.*

Most writing occurs in the **past tense,** either simple or perfect. When telling about two events that occurred in the past, the more recent event is written in the simple past tense, and the earlier event is written in the past perfect tense.

The soldiers *cried* (past tense) because they *had lost* (past perfect) their gifts.

Simple past is commonly called *past*; simple present, *present*; and simple future, *future.*

Forms of *have* include *have, has,* and *had.*

Use *had* + the past participle of a verb to form the past perfect.

Voice

Verb voice indicates if the subject is doing or receiving the action. There are two voices in English: active and passive.

In **active voice**, the subject of the sentence is doing the verb action. The active voice creates a strong image and feeling because it highlights the doer of the action. Most sentences should be written in active voice.

Will climbed the tree.
The subject (Will) is doing the verb (climbed).

In **passive voice**, the subject receives the action of the verb. The subject is not doing any action. The verb is always in the form of a verb phrase (two or more words) that contains a *be* verb and a past participle. Because the passive voice is often wordy and dull, avoid overusing the passive voice.

The *tree was climbed* by Will. The *tree was climbed.*
In both sentences the subject (the tree) is not doing the verb action (was climbed). Someone or something else is doing the verb action. In the first sentence who is doing the verb is specified (Will). In the second sentence it is implied.

Action verbs, not linking verbs, can be passive or active.

To create a strong image and feeling, write sentences where the subject actively does the verb action.

Sam kicked the ball is better than *The ball was kicked by Sam.*

Advanced

PATTERN subject (person/thing being acted on) **+ be verb + past participle + by someone or something** (either in the sentence or implied). The passive sentence must have all four elements.

The tree (thing being acted on) was (be verb) climbed (past participle) by Will (by someone).
The castle (the thing being acted on) would be (be verb) demolished (past participle) by the soldiers (by someone).

Understanding passive voice helps distinguish if an -ed word is operating as a verb or an adjective.

The sandwich (the thing being acted on) was (be verb) devoured (past participle).
Someone must have devoured the sandwich, so the "by someone" is implied.
Since this sentence follows the passive voice pattern, *devoured* is a verb.

Molly (subject) was (be verb) famished (-ed word).
Since *famished* is a state of being, not something being done to Molly, there is no implied "by someone" phrase. Thus, *famished* is an adjective that follows a linking verb (was), describing Molly.

Mood

Verb mood indicates how an action is expressed, telling if it is a fact, opinion, command, or suggestion. There are three moods in English: indicative, imperative, and subjunctive.

The **indicative mood** makes statements or asks questions.

I will swim. Will you swim with me?

The **imperative mood** gives a command or makes a request. The subject of an imperative sentence is always *you.*

Swim. Swim to the other side of the pond.

The **subjunctive mood** expresses contrary-to-fact conditions with *wish* or *if* statements in the third person. It is used infrequently.

If Sam were concerned, he would take swimming lessons.
Sam is not concerned, so the subjunctive *Sam were* is correct.

Sam's mother wishes that he were a stronger swimmer.
Sam is not a stronger swimmer, so the subjunctive *he were* is correct.

Conjunction

A conjunction connects words, phrases, or clauses.

A **coordinating conjunction** connects the same type of words, phrases, or clauses. The items the coordinating conjunction connects must be grammatically the same: two or more nouns, two or more present participles, two or more dependent clauses, two or more main clauses, and so forth.

Memorize the cc's using the acronym FANBOYS: *for, and, nor, but, or, yet, so.*

There are seven coordinating conjunctions: *for, and, nor, but, or, yet, so.*

Use a comma before a coordinating conjunction when it connects three or more items in a series.
PATTERN a, b, and c

He *ran* to the window**,** *opened* it**,** and *jumped* out.

Use a comma before a coordinating conjunction when it connects two main clauses (a compound sentence).
PATTERN MC, cc MC

The *cook yelled***,** and the *mouse ran.*

Do not use a comma before a coordinating conjunction when it connects two items in a series unless they are main clauses.
PATTERN a and b

The cook saw the *vegetables* (no comma) but not the *mouse.*

Do not use a comma before a coordinating conjunction when it connects two verbs (a compound verb) with the same subject.
PATTERN MC cc 2nd verb

The cook *yelled* (no comma) and *ran.*

Starting sentences with a coordinating conjunction is discouraged in formal writing on the basis that a coordinating conjunction connects things of equal grammatical construction within a sentence.

In academic papers students should avoid beginning a sentence with a cc.

In fictional papers dialogue can mimic real speech patterns. Thoughts often begin with *and* or *but*.

Faulty parallelism occurs when a coordinating conjunction does not connect things of equal grammatical construction. This means that the items in a series are not parallel.

He *ran* to the window, *opened* it, and *jumping* out.
Ran, opened, and jumping are not the same verb form. To correct, change jumping to jumped: He *ran, opened,* and *jumped.*

A **subordinating conjunction** (also called a www word) usually connects an adverb clause to a main clause. The adverb clause is a dependent clause, which cannot stand alone as a sentence. It begins with a www word and contains a subject and a verb.

PATTERN

www word + subject + verb

There are many subordinating conjunctions. The most common are taught using the acronym ***www.asia.b***: when, while, where, as, since, if, although, because. Other words function as subordinating conjunctions: after, before, until, unless, whenever, whereas, than.

Memorize the most common www words using the acronym *www.asia.b:* when, while, where, as, since, if, although, because.

Use a comma after an adverb clause that comes before a main clause.
PATTERN AC, MC

When it rained, Timmy stayed indoors.

Do not use a comma before an adverb clause.
PATTERN MC AC

Timmy stayed indoors (no comma) *when it rained.*

A word functions as a subordinating conjunction only when it is followed by a subject and verb. This is why recognizing the pattern www word + subject + verb is important. If a verb is not present, the group of words is likely a prepositional phrase and not a clause. See pages G-18 and G-21.

A **conjunctive adverb** connects ideas or provides a transition.

Common conjunctive adverbs are *however, therefore, then, moreover, consequently, otherwise, nevertheless, thus, furthermore, instead, otherwise.*

Place commas around a conjunctive adverb if it interrupts the flow of the sentence. The exception is one-syllable conjunctive adverbs like *then.*

Moreover, Robin Hood had many followers.
Robin Hood was a talented archer and, *moreover*, a good leader.
Then (no comma) he took an arrow from his quiver.

If a conjunctive adverb is used to connect two main clauses that express similar ideas, place a semicolon before the conjunctive adverb and a comma after.
PATTERN MC; ca, MC.

The outlaws lived in the forest; *however*, the forest belonged to the king.

When you add a conjunctive adverb to a main clause, it is still a main clause, which is not the case with subordinating conjunctions or relative pronouns.

Adjective

An **adjective** describes a noun or pronoun. An adjective tells which one, what kind, how many, or whose.

An adjective comes before the noun it describes or follows a linking verb and describes the subject. See page G-9.

The scared mice jumped from the first basket and ran under the cook's feet.
What kind of mice? *scared* Which basket? *first* Whose feet? *cook's*

The mice appeared *scared*.
Scared follows *appeared* (linking verb) and describes *mice* (subject).

An **article adjective** signals a noun is coming. The article adjectives are *a, an, the.* Sometimes adjectives come between the article and its noun.

The tall stranger entered *the* room.

The boy appeared to be *a* reluctant, timid soldier.

A **comparative adjective** is formed by adding the adverb *more* or the ending *-er* to an adjective. A comparative adjective compares two nouns.

The rose was *more* beautiful than the daisy.

The boy stood *taller* than his mother.

A **superlative adjective** is formed by adding the adverb *most* or the ending *-est* to an adjective. A superlative adjective compares three or more nouns.

This is the *most* interesting book I have read.

The Little Mermaid was the *youngest* in her family.

Most one-syllable adjectives form the comparative and superlative by adding the suffix *-er* or *-est*. Three or more syllable adjectives form the comparative with *more* and the superlative with *most*. Two-syllable adjectives are formed both ways. If in doubt, consult a dictionary.

Use a comma to separate **coordinate adjectives.** Adjectives are coordinate if each adjective independently describes the noun that follows. The order is not important.

The woman had a thin face with a pointed**,** protruding nose.
It sounds right to say both *protruding, pointed nose* and *pointed and protruding nose*. The adjectives are coordinate and the comma is necessary.

Do not use a comma to separate **cumulative adjectives.** Adjectives are cumulative if the first adjective describes the second adjective and the noun that follows. Cumulative adjectives follow this specific order: quantity, opinion, size, age, shape, color, origin, material, purpose.

Robin saw fifteen foresters seated beneath a huge oak tree.
It does not sound right to say *oak huge tree* or *huge and oak tree.*
The adjectives are cumulative and should not have a comma.

A **possessive adjective** is a noun functioning as an adjective in order to show ownership. See page G-28.

The vest belonged to Timmy (noun).

Timmy's (possessive adjective) vest had several pockets.

Adjective Test:
the _______ pen

Which pen?
the *first* pen
that pen

What kind of pen?
a *shiny* pen
the *green* pen

How many pens?
twenty pens
few pens

Whose pen?
the *teacher's* pen
my pen

Some words form irregular comparatives and superlatives. The most common of these are *good, better, best* and *bad, worse, worst.*

Only coordinate adjectives need to be separated with a comma.

Adjectives are coordinate if you can reverse their order or add *and* between them.

Adjectives are cumulative if they must be arranged in a specific order.

Adverb

An **adverb** modifies a verb, an adjective, or another adverb. An adverb tells how, when, where, why, or to what extent.

I dropped the pen there beside the book.
Dropped where? *there*

He seemed genuinely happy when he indicated that he would visit us later.
How happy? *genuinely* Visit when? *later*

An **-ly adverb** is an adverb that ends in -ly. Not all words that end in -ly are adverbs. Impostor -ly adverbs are adjectives like *chilly, ghastly, ugly,* and *friendly*. If the word ending in -ly describes a noun, it is an adjective and not an adverb.

Inadvertently Frederick touched Dorinda's omelet with his hind leg.
Touched how? *inadvertently* Inadvertently is an adverb.

Dorinda accidentally hurled him across the room.
Hurled how? *accidentally* Accidentally is an adverb.

Frederick uttered a ghastly sound when his leg broke.
What kind of sound? *ghastly* Ghastly is not an -ly adverb. It is an adjective because it describes the noun *sound.*

An **interrogative adverb** is an adverb used to begin a question. The interrogative adverbs are *how, when, where,* and *why.*

Why do bees sting, Baloo?

How will you collect the honey?

A **comparative** or **superlative** adverb is usually formed by adding the adverbs *more* or *most* in front of the adverb. If the adverb is short, the suffix *-er* or *-est* is used, as in faster or fastest. If in doubt, consult a dictionary.

Do not place *more* or *most* before the word with *-er* or *-est* after. Not *more faster* but *faster.*

Interjection

An **interjection** expresses an emotion.

When an interjection expresses a strong emotion, use an exclamation mark. The next word begins with a capital letter.

Help! My golden ball has vanished.

When an interjection does not express a strong emotion, use a comma.

Oh, I see it now.

The Sentence

Sentences are essential to writing. As the building blocks of sentences, clauses and phrases are the most important structural units of language. For the reader, the ability to recognize clauses and phrases results in greater comprehension. For the writer, the ability to organize clauses and phrases results in clearer communication. The writer must know enough about each to punctuate properly. This section defines these terms and explains the related commas rules.

Sentence

A sentence contains a subject and a verb and expresses one complete thought.

Every sentence must have a main clause.

A sentence begins with a capital letter and ends with an end mark. It contains at least one subject-verb pair, which is called a main clause. A **subject** is the noun or pronoun that tells who or what the clause is about. A **verb** tells what the subject is doing. Additional words, phrases, and clauses may be added.

A **run-on** occurs when a sentence has two main clauses that are not connected properly. There are two types of run-ons, which are always wrong.

A **fused sentence** is two main clauses placed in one sentence without any punctuation between them. **MC MC.**

Quinn glanced up the door slammed shut.

A **comma splice** is two main clauses placed in one sentence with only a comma between them. **MC, MC.**

Quinn glanced up, the door slammed shut.

A period is usually the easiest solution for run-ons.

A semicolon is only used when both main clauses are closely related and usually parallel in construction.

There are four main ways to fix a run-on.

1. Period: Quinn glanced up**.** The door slammed shut**.** **PATTERN MC. MC.**
2. Comma + cc: Quinn glanced up**,** *and* the door slammed shut. **PATTERN MC, cc MC.**
3. Adverb clause: Start one of the clauses with one of the www words.

   As Quinn glanced up**,** the door slammed shut. **PATTERN AC, MC.**

   Quinn glanced up *as* the door slammed shut. **PATTERN MC AC.**
4. Semicolon: Quinn glanced up**;** the door slammed shut. **PATTERN MC; MC.**

Of these options for this example, the adverb clause is the best solution because *as* explains how the two clauses are related.

A **fragment** occurs when a sentence does not contain a main clause. The group of words may contain a phrase and/or a dependent clause, but it is only part of a sentence.

Fragments that do not leave the reader hanging and that fit the flow of the paragraph are dramatic and effective. *Fix It!* stories permit such fragments, especially in dialogue.

Timmy saw his dear friend. (sentence)
Greeting him kindly. (unacceptable fragment)
"Hello, Johnny!" (acceptable fragment)

Phrase

A phrase is a group of related words that contains either a noun or a verb, never both.

A **prepositional phrase** begins with a preposition and ends with a noun. There might be other words between the preposition and the noun, but there is never a verb in a prepositional phrase.

PATTERN

preposition + noun (no verb)

To identify a prepositional phrase, find a word that appears to be a preposition and ask *what*? Answer with a noun, never a verb. See page G-8.

Through the glimmering twilight beamed the evening star in all its beauty.
Find a preposition. *through* through what? *through the glimmering twilight*
Find a preposition. *in* in what? *in all its beauty*

If a prepositional opener has five words or more, follow it with a comma.

Under the table (no comma) the tiny mouse hid.

Under the heavy wooden table, the tiny mouse hid.

If two or more prepositional phrases open a sentence, follow the last phrase with a comma.

Under the heavy wooden table in the kitchen, the tiny mouse hid.

If a prepositional opener functions as a transition, follow it with a comma.

Of course, the cook was afraid of mice.

Prepositional phrases that function as transitions require commas.

in fact
in addition
by the way
by contrast
for example
for instance
of course
on the other hand

If a prepositional opener is followed by a main clause that has the verb before the subject, do not use a comma.

Under the heavy wooden table hid a tiny mouse.

Do not put a comma in front of a prepositional phrase unless the phrase is a transition.

The mouse hid (no comma) *under a table in the kitchen.*

The cook was, *of course*, afraid of mice.

Recognizing the basic clause and phrase structure of a sentence will allow students to punctuate their sentences properly. Removing prepositional phrases helps reveal the underlying structure of the sentence.

When a prepositional phrase is misplaced, the meaning is distorted, often humorously. Revise the sentence by moving the prepositional phrase.

The mouse hid under a table with the long gray tail.

The mouse, not the table, has the long gray tail.

The mouse with the long gray tail hid under a table.

Advanced

When a preposition ends a sentence, it is not wrong. This is a carryover from Latin and not a true rule in English. Andrew Pudewa quips that Winston Churchill gave the definitive answer to this problem when he remarked, "That is a rule up with which I will not put!" If the sentence is more awkward to revise with the preposition placed earlier, it is better to have it at the end.

I have only a staff to meet you with.

The alternative is this stilted construction: I have only a staff with which to meet you.

A **verb phrase** is one main verb (action or linking) and one or more helping verbs. The helping verb indicates the tense, mood, and voice. Sometimes the helping verb(s) and the main verb are separated by other words. See page G-9.

Every clause must have an action or a linking verb, not a helping verb.

The Little Mermaid *could* (helping verb) not *forget* (action verb) the charming prince.
The verb phrase *could forget* functions as the verb.

A **participial phrase** begins with a participle (verb + -ing or -ed) and includes its modifiers and complements. A participial phrase functions as an adjective that describes a noun in the sentence.

A #4 -ing opener is a participial opener. See page G-44.

Springing to his feet, Robin Hood confronted the challenger.
Springing to his feet describes Robin Hood, the subject of the main clause.

Robin Hood, *thinking of Maid Marian,* whistled merrily.
Thinking of Maid Marian describes Robin Hood, the subject of the main clause.

Affronted by their mockery, Robin challenged the foresters.
Affronted by their mockery describes Robin, the subject of the main clause.

The path brought them to a broad stream *spanned by a narrow bridge.*
Spanned by a narrow bridge describes stream, the object of the prepositional phrase.

Use a comma after a participial opener (-ing), even if it is short.
PATTERN **-ing word/phrase, main clause**

Gathering their three gifts, the soldiers visited the king.
The thing after the comma is the thing doing the inging.

Place commas around a mid-sentence participial phrase if it is nonessential to the meaning of the sentence.

David, *playing on the beach*, saw a mermaid. (nonessential, commas)
The proper noun David defines which child saw a mermaid.

Use a comma when a participial phrase comes at the end of a sentence and describes a noun other than the word it follows.

Robin whistled, *thinking of Maid Marian.* (describes Robin, comma)

Do not place commas around a mid-sentence participial phrase if it is essential to the meaning of the sentence. See page G-26.

The child *playing on the beach* saw a mermaid. (essential, no commas)
The phrase is essential because it defines which child saw a mermaid.

Do not use a comma when a participial phrase comes at the end of a sentence and describes the word it follows.

Dorinda saw her ball rolling down the hill. (describes ball, no comma)

Clause

A clause is a group of related words that contains both a subject and a verb.

A **main clause [MC]** has a subject and a verb. A main clause, sometimes called an independent clause, can stand alone as a sentence because it expresses a complete thought.

The second solider took the road to the right. [main clause]

A **dependent clause** also has a subject and a verb. However, it cannot stand alone as a sentence because it does not express a complete thought. As a result, a dependent clause, sometimes called a subordinate clause, must be added to a main clause to make sense. Dependent clauses begin with a word that causes them to be an incomplete thought.

Although the second soldier took the road to the right. (dependent clause)

One of the keys to punctuating sentences properly is being able to identify dependent clauses accurately. Every dependent clause functions as either an adjective, an adverb, or a noun.

Identify the clause by 1) focusing on the word that begins the dependent clause and 2) checking the placement of the clause in the sentence. Once the clause function has been determined, properly punctuating the sentence is easy.

Contains:
subject + verb

stands alone

Contains:
subject + verb

cannot stand alone

Main Clause [MC]

subject + verb
stands alone

[The frog rescued her ball.]

Dependent Clause

subject + verb
cannot stand alone

Adjective Dependent Clause

[The frog, (who was actually a prince,) rescued her ball.]

who/which clause (*w/w*)
functions as an adjective
begins with *who, which, that*
use commas unless essential

Adverb Dependent Clause

(When her ball fell into the well,) [the frog rescued it.]

[The frog rescued her ball] (when it fell into the well.)

www.asia.b clause (AC)
functions as an adverb
begins with www word
use comma after but not before

Noun Dependent Clause

[Dorinda did not realize] (that the frog was a prince.)

that clause (that)
functions as a noun
often begins with *that*
no commas

An **adjective clause** is a dependent clause that functions as an adjective.

Because the adjective clause is a dependent clause, it must be added to a main clause. Most of the time it directly follows the noun or pronoun that it describes.

An adjective clause begins with a relative pronoun (*who, which, that*) or a relative adverb (*where, when, why*) and contains both a subject and a verb. The subject of the adjective clause is often the word it begins with (such as *who, which, where*). See page G-6.

Robin, who lived among them, led the outlaws.
Robin led the outlaws is the main clause.
(*Robin* is the subject; *led* is the verb.)

Who lived among them is the adjective clause.
(*Who* is the subject; *lived* is the verb.)

Place commas around an adjective clause if it is nonessential to the meaning of the sentence.

Robin**,** *who was happy and carefree***,** traveled through the forest. (nonessential, commas)

Do not place commas around an adjective clause if it is essential to the meaning of the sentence. See page G-26.

The men *who followed Robin Hood* could be trusted. (essential, no commas) The clause is essential because it defines which men could be trusted.

The *who/which* clause is an adjective clause that begins with *who* or *which*. See page G-39.

An adjective clause that begins with *that* is always essential. Thus, *that* clauses do not take commas.

Advanced

A relative pronoun introduces the adjective clause and connects it to the main clause. It functions as a pronoun because it replaces the noun or pronoun that precedes it.

The woman served brown bread, ~~bread~~ *which* tasted delicious.

An **adverb clause** is a dependent clause that functions as an adverb.

Because the adverb clause is a dependent clause, it must be added to a main clause. An adverb clause may appear anywhere in a sentence.

An adverb clause begins with a subordinating conjunction (www word) and contains both a subject and a verb. See page G-13.

PATTERN

www word + subject + verb

Eden admired Quinn while she sang her solo.
Eden admired Quinn is the main clause.
(*Eden* is the subject; *admired* is the verb.)

While she sang her solo is the adverb clause.
(*She* is the subject; *sang* is the verb.)

Use a comma after an adverb clause that comes before a main clause.
PATTERN AC, MC

*When it rained***,** Timmy stayed indoors.

Do not use a comma before an adverb clause.
PATTERN MC AC

Timmy stayed indoors (no comma) *when it rained*.

A comma is placed before *although*, *while*, or *whereas* when a strong contrast exists. See page G-26.

An adverb clause follows the pattern www word + subject + verb. If a verb is not present, the group of words is likely a prepositional phrase. See page G-18.

A **noun clause** is a dependent clause that functions as a noun.

A noun clause can do any function that a noun can do: subject, object of the preposition, direct object, indirect object, subject complement. See page G-7.

Like the other dependent clauses, the noun clause contains both a subject and a verb. Many noun clauses begin with *that,* but they can also begin with other words, including *how, what, when, where, whether, which, who, why.*

What Dorinda said disappointed her father.
What Dorinda said is the subject of the main clause.

Dorinda did not realize *when her actions were unacceptable.*
When her actions were unacceptable is the direct object of the verb *realize.*

Dorinda's primary problem was *that she was self-centered.*
That she was self-centered is the subject complement.

An invisible noun clause occurs when the word *that* is implied, not stated directly.

Dorinda never seemed to understand [that] she was responsible.
She was responsible is the direct object of the verbal *to understand. That* is implied.

Frederick could tell [that] he would enjoy his stay.
He would enjoy his stay is the direct object of the verb *could tell. That* is implied.

The advanced dress-up noun clause is a noun clause that begins with *that.* See page G-41.

Both noun clauses and adjective clauses can begin with the word *that.*

If *which* can be substituted for *that,* the *that* clause is an adjective clause.

Noun clauses do not take commas.

People felt (no comma) *that Robin Hood was like them.*

Robin Hood was pleased (no comma) *that he had escaped.*

Advanced

The first word of a dependent clause does not always indicate the type of clause. The word *that* can begin both adjective clauses and noun clauses. The words *where, when,* and *why* can begin adjective, adverb, and noun clauses. Accurate identification requires one to consider the way the entire clause is functioning in the sentence.

The Little Mermaid determined to look *where the prince now lived with his bride.*
The dependent clause begins with *where* and tells the location of where the Little Mermaid looked.
This is an adverb clause, so a comma is not needed.

The Little Mermaid noticed the sky, *where the rosy dawn glimmered more and more brightly.*
The dependent clauses begins with *where* and directly follows the noun *sky.*
This is a nonessential adjective clause, so a comma is needed.

Punctuation

End Marks . ? !

Period

Use a period at the end of a statement.

He bowed and walked away.

Use a period with some abbreviations.

ea. st. Mrs.

Question Mark

Use a question mark at the end of a question.

Did you ever hear the story of the three poor soldiers?

Exclamation Mark

Use an exclamation mark at the end of a sentence that expresses strong emotion.

No one calls me a coward!

Use an exclamation mark after an interjection that expresses strong emotion.

Yuck! I won't touch another bite.

Use only one end mark.

"You're sure?" "Hah!" he said. (correct)

"You're sure?!" "Hah!," he said. (incorrect)

Commas ,

Adjectives before a Noun

Use a comma to separate **coordinate adjectives**. Adjectives are coordinate if each adjective independently describes the noun that follows. The order is not important.

The woman had a pointed**,** protruding nose.
It sounds right to say both *protruding, pointed nose* and *pointed and protruding nose.*
The adjectives are coordinate and the comma is necessary.

Do not use a comma to separate **cumulative adjectives**. Adjectives are cumulative if the first adjective describes the second adjective and the noun that follows. Cumulative adjectives follow this specific order: quantity, opinion, size, age, shape, color, origin, material, purpose.

The soldiers reached the tall green gate.
It does not sound right to say *green tall gate* or *tall and green gate.*
The adjectives are cumulative and should not have a comma.

Only coordinate adjectives need to be separated with a comma.

Adjectives are coordinate if you can reverse their order or add *and* between them.

Adjectives are cumulative if they must be arranged in a specific order.

Noun of Direct Address (NDA)

Place commas around a noun of direct address. See page G-7.

*My friends***,** for fourteen days we have enjoyed no sport.

For fourteen days**,** *my friends***,** we have enjoyed no sport.

For fourteen days we have enjoyed no sport**,** *my friends.*

Items in a Series

PATTERN a, b, and c Use commas to separate three or more items in a series. Place the final comma before the coordinating conjunction. These items must be grammatically the same.

He *ran* to the window**,** *opened* it**,** and *jumped* out.

The cook removed the *tomatoes***,** *beans***,** and *cucumbers.*

PATTERN a and b Do not use a comma before a coordinating conjunction when it connects two items in a series unless they are main clauses.

The cook removed the *tomatoes* (no comma) and *cucumbers.*

The cook *yelled* (no comma) and *ran.*

The Oxford Comma is the comma before the coordinating conjunction in three or more items in a series. Although the Oxford comma is optional if there is no danger of misreading, writers do not always recognize potential confusion. It is wise to include it since the addition of the Oxford Comma is rarely wrong.

Compound Verb

PATTERN MC cc 2nd verb Do not use a comma before a coordinating conjunction when it connects two verbs (a compound verb) with the same subject. There is no subject after the cc.

The cook *yelled* (no comma) and *ran.*

He *ran* to the window (no comma) and *opened* it.

This is the same as pattern a and b.

Compound Sentence

PATTERN MC, cc MC Use a comma before a coordinating conjunction when it connects two main clauses (a compound sentence). There is a subject and a verb after the cc.

The *cook yelled***,** and the *mouse ran.*

He ran to the window**,** and *he opened* it.

The comma in the MC, cc MC pattern is optional when the clauses are short and there is no danger of misreading.

Mid-Sentence Prepositional Phrase

Do not put a comma in front of a prepositional phrase unless the phrase is a transition.

The mouse hid (no comma) *under a table in the kitchen.*

The cook was**,** *of course***,** afraid of mice.

Prepositional Phrase Opener (#2 Sentence Opener)

If a prepositional opener has five words or more, follow it with a comma.

Under the table (no comma) the tiny mouse hid.

Under the heavy wooden table, the tiny mouse hid.

If two or more prepositional phrases open a sentence, follow the last phrase with a comma.

Under the heavy wooden table in the kitchen, the tiny mouse hid.

If a prepositional opener functions as a transition, follow it with a comma.

Of course, the cook was afraid of mice.

If a prepositional opener is followed by a main clause that has the verb before the subject, do not use a comma.

Under the heavy wooden table hid a tiny mouse.

Prepositional phrases that work as transitions and require commas include

in fact
in addition
by the way
by contrast
for example
for instance
of course
on the other hand

Transition and Interrupter

Place commas around a transition and an interrupter.

Of course, Dorinda and Maribella lived in the castle.

As grown-up girls they could, *on the other hand*, leave when they pleased.

They rarely left the palace grounds, *however*.

When transitional words connect two main clauses, put a semicolon before and a comma after. See page G-29.

-ly Adverb Opener (#3 Sentence Opener)

Use a comma if an -ly adverb opener modifies the sentence.

Foolishly, Timmy bit into a hot pepper.
Test: It was foolish that Timmy bit ... makes sense. *Foolishly* modifies the sentence.

Do not use a comma if an -ly adverb opener modifies the verb.

Eagerly Timmy ate a ripe cucumber.
Test: It was eager that Timmy ate ... does not make sense. *Eagerly* modifies the verb *ate*.

Test:

It was ___ that ___.

End-Sentence Participial Phrase

Do not use a comma when the participial phrase (-ing) describes the word directly before it.

Dorinda saw her ball (no comma) *rolling down the hill.*

Robin Hood whistled, *thinking of Maid Marian.*

Participial Phrase Opener (#4 Sentence Opener)

Use a comma after a participial opener (-ing), even if it is short.

Excusing herself from the table, Dorinda hurried away.

Adverb Clause Opener (#5 Sentence Opener)

PATTERN AC, MC Use a comma after an adverb clause opener.

When the cat prowled at night, the mice hid.

Mid-Sentence Adverb Clause

PATTERN AC, MC Use a comma after an adverb clause that comes before a main clause.

Early that morning *when Timmy saw the cat*, he was aghast.

PATTERN MC AC Do not use a comma before an adverb clause.

Early that morning Timmy was aghast (no comma) *when he saw the cat.*

Quotation

Use a comma to separate an attribution from a direct quote.

A throaty voice offered, "I should be honored to find your ball."

"I should be honored," a throaty voice offered, "to find your ball."

"I should be honored to find your ball," a throaty voice offered.

The attribution is the narrative that includes the person speaking and the speaking verb (*he said*).

Comparing Items

Do not use a comma when making a comparison.

Robin was a better shot (no comma) *than the other archers.*

Contrasting Items

Use a comma to separate contrasting parts of a sentence.

The ideas in this story are the rooster's thoughts, *not mine.*

Use a comma even if the contrasting part begins with www words *although, while,* or *whereas.* This rule applies only when there is an extreme contrast and is an exception to **MC AC**.

He seemed interested, *whereas* she did not.

Timmy favored the country, *while* Johnny preferred the city.

Use a comma to contrast, not compare.

Appositive, Adjective Clause, Mid-Sentence Participial Phrase

A nonessential appositive, adjective clause, or mid-sentence participial phrase adds information to a sentence.

Use commas to separate nonessential elements from the rest of the sentence.

Robin Hood, *the archer,* led his men through the forest.

Little John, *who liked a challenge,* readily followed Robin.

The men, *laughing at each other,* hiked through the forest.

An essential appositive, adjective clause, or mid-sentence participial phrase defines the noun it follows. If the essential information is removed, the overall meaning of the sentence changes.

Do not use commas with essential elements.

The archer *Robin Hood* led his men through the forest.

The men *who followed Robin Hood* could be trusted.

The man *walking across the bridge* was a stranger.

An appositive is an invisible *who/which* clause. See page G-39.

A *who/which* clause is an adjective clause.

A participial phrase is an -ing phrase.

To determine if a phrase or clause is essential, remove it from the sentence to see if it changes the meaning of the sentence.

Little John, *who liked a challenge,* readily followed Robin.
Remove the *who/which* clause: Little John readily followed Robin. This does not change the meaning of the sentence. This *who* clause is nonessential. Use commas.

The men *who followed Robin Hood* could be trusted.
Remove the *who/which* clause: The men could be trusted. This changes the meaning because the reader does not know which men could be trusted. This *who* clause is essential. Do not use commas.

Nonessential items need commas.

Essential items eliminate commas.

In some cases, the commas determine the meaning of the sentence.

Even the footmen, *who once obeyed her,* snubbed her.
With commas this sentence indicates all footmen snubbed her and all once obeyed her.

Even the footmen *who once obeyed her* snubbed her.
Without commas this same sentence now indicates that only those footmen who once obeyed her now snubbed her.

Quotation Marks “ ”

Direct Quotation

Use quotation marks to enclose direct quotations.

“I want to live above the sea,” said the Little Mermaid.

There should not be a space between the quotation mark and the word or punctuation it encloses.

Indirect Quotation

Do not use quotation marks with indirect speech, which usually begins with *that.*

The Little Mermaid said that she wanted to live above the sea.

Thoughts

When typing, place thoughts in italics. When handwriting, use quotation marks.

I do not want a fish's tail, thought the Little Mermaid.

Punctuating a Quotation

Use a comma to separate an attribution from a direct quote. If a direct quote is an exclamation or question, follow it with an exclamation or question mark.

The attribution is the narrative that includes the person speaking and the speaking verb (*he said*).

Attribution, “Quote.”	Attribution, “Quote!”	Attribution, “Quote?”
“Quote,” attribution.	“Quote!” attribution.	“Quote?” attribution.

Commas and periods always go inside closing quotation marks.

“I want to live above the sea,” said the Little Mermaid.

Hans Christian Andersen wrote “The Little Mermaid.”

Exclamation marks and question marks go inside closing quotations when they are part of the quoted material; otherwise, they go outside.

“Can humans live forever?” the Little Mermaid asked.

Did Grandmother say, “Humans can live forever”?

When a spoken sentence is interrupted, close the first part and begin the second with quotation marks. Do not capitalize the first letter of the continuation.

“Human beings have a soul,” explained Grandmother, “that lives eternally.”

In conversation, if someone speaking changes topic, start a new paragraph. Close the first paragraph without a quotation mark to signal the speaker has not finished speaking. Open the new paragraph with a quotation mark to indicate that someone is still speaking.

The prince responded, “You remind me of a girl I once met.

“Long ago, my ship wrecked, and the waves cast me ashore. A maiden saved my life.”

Referencing Words

When typing, place words referred to as words in italics or quotation marks. When handwriting, use quotation marks.

The king believed *sir* and *madam* should be used when addressing one's elders.

Insert “the word(s)” or “the name” before the word in question to tell if this rule applies.

Single Quotation Marks

Use single quotation marks for quotations within quotations.

The maid said, “Strip the mattresses since, as the queen put it, ‘They might be unclean.’”

This is the only reason to use single quotation marks.

Apostrophes ’

Contraction

Use an apostrophe to show where a letter or letters have been removed.

I’ll figure out how to trick them.

It’s too bad, but we’d better go our separate ways.

Possessive Adjective

Use an apostrophe to show possession.

To form singular possessives, add an apostrophe + *s*.

the second soldier’s turn

To form plural possessives, make the noun plural; then add an apostrophe.

the soldiers’ last night at the palace (the last night of all three soldiers)

An exception is irregular plural possessives.

the children’s mittens and the women’s scarves

Plural Noun

Do not use an apostrophe to make a word plural.

The *soldiers* each took a turn.

The *princesses* received whatever they requested.

Possessive Pronoun

Do not use an apostrophe with possessive pronouns.

his, hers, its, theirs, ours, yours

Possessive Pronouns	Contractions
its	it’s (it is)
their	they’re (they are)
theirs	there’s (there is)
whose	who’s (who is)

Ellipsis Points ...

Fictional Writing

Use ellipsis points to signal hesitation or a reflective pause, especially in dialogue.

“Ahem **...** ” Lord Ashton cleared his throat conspicuously.

“Um **...** certainly **...** the mattress test,” the king sighed.

Nonfictional Writing

Use ellipses only when omitting words from a direct quotation.

Semicolons ;

Main Clauses

PATTERN MC; MC Use a semicolon to join main clauses that are closely related and parallel in construction.

The Little Mermaid pondered golden sunsets**;** she dreamed of twinkling stars.

Conjunctive Adverb

PATTERN MC; ca, MC. If a conjunctive adverb is used to connect two main clauses that express similar ideas, put a semicolon before the conjunctive adverb and a comma after.

Conjunctive adverbs are transition words.

Years of indulgence had spoiled her beyond recognition**;** *however***,** Lady Constance recalled a time in Dorinda's childhood when she had been a lovable child.

Items in a Series

Use semicolons to separate items in a series when the items contain internal commas.

Highborn women lamented when Troy, that noble city celebrated by Homer, fell through trickery**;** when Pyrrhus, ancient Greek ruler, seized King Priam by the beard**;** and when the Romans, ruthless and crazed, torched Carthage to the ground.

Colons :

List

Colons follow a complete thought and mean *see what follows* or *an example follows.*

PATTERN MC: list Use a colon after a main clause to introduce a list when a phrase like *for example* is not included.

Robin Hood had two choices**:** run away or fight.

Explanation

PATTERN MC: explanation Use a colon after a main clause to introduce an explanation when a phrase like *for example* is not included.

One other thing I ask**:** please accept this simple souvenir from me.

Quotation

Contrast this with an attribution. The innkeeper answered, "Sir, your friend left town at dawn."

PATTERN MC: quotation Use a colon when a complete thought sets up a quotation.

The innkeeper answered him straightaway**:** "Sir, your friend left town at dawn."

Titles with Subtitles

PATTERN Title: Subtitle Use a colon to separate a title from a subtitle.

Charles Dickens wrote *Oliver Twist***:** *The Parish Boy's Progress* and *A Christmas Carol***:** *A Ghost Story of Christmas.*

Hyphens -

Numbers

Use a hyphen with compound numbers from twenty-one to ninety-nine and with fractions.

thirty-seven; one-fourth

Compound Nouns

Use hyphens with some compound nouns.

lady-in-waiting; mother-in-law; self-restraint

Compound Adjectives

Use a hyphen when two or more words come before a noun they describe and act as a single idea.

The *nineteenth-century* author enjoyed his fame.

The *five-year-old* boy cried.

When a compound adjective follows the noun it describes, the adjective may or may not be hyphenated. If in doubt, consult a dictionary.

The boy was *five years old.*

Mowgli was *self-confident.*

Em Dashes and Parentheses — ( )

Emphasis

Use em dashes to emphasize something.

Your word—of all people's—must be trustworthy.

Use em dashes in place of commas when you want to draw attention to something.

Interruption

Use em dashes to indicate an interruption in speech or a sudden break in thought.

His younger daughter—now there was another topic that brought red to his face—embarrassed him in front of the guests.

Use parentheses in place of commas when you want to offer an aside.

Nonessential Elements

Use em dashes to set off nonessential elements that have commas inside them.

The poor widow owned a few farm animals—three hefty sows, three cows, and a sheep dubbed Molly—with which she attempted to eke out a living.

Extra Information

Use parentheses to provide extra information.

"Oh, yes, benevolent frog!" (Notice that in fairy tales, characters don't have great curiosity about such oddities as talking frogs.)

Additional Concepts

Indentation

In copy work, indent by doing two things: 1) start on the next line, and 2) start writing ½ inch from the left margin.

The paragraph mark (¶) is called a pilcrow.

To mark indentation, add the ¶ symbol or an arrow (➔) in front of each sentence that should start a new paragraph.

In fiction (stories), there are four reasons to start a new paragraph.

New Speaker

Start a new paragraph when a new character speaks. Include the attribution with the quotation.

> She cried loudly, "Thieves!"

If a narrative sentence sets up the quotation, it should go in the same paragraph as the quoted sentence.

> The stranger came right to the point. "It is cowardly to stand there with a lethal arrow aimed at my heart."

If a narrative follows a quotation in a separate sentence but points directly back to the quotation, it can also go in the same paragraph.

> "It is cowardly to stand there with a lethal arrow aimed at my heart." The stranger did not mince words.

New Topic

Start a new paragraph when the narrator or a character switches topic or focus.

New Place

Start a new paragraph when the story switches to a new location. If several switches are made in quick succession, such as a character's journey to find something, it may be less choppy to keep in one paragraph.

New Time

Start a new paragraph when the time changes unless there are several time shifts in close succession that make sense together in a single paragraph.

Capitalization

Sentence

Capitalize the first word of a sentence and of a quoted sentence, even when it does not begin the full sentence.

The princess cried, "**M**y nose has grown too long."

Do not capitalize the first word of an attribution when it follows the quoted sentence.

"My nose has grown too long," **t**he princess cried.

"You must be content!" **u**rged grandmother

Quotation Continues

When a spoken sentence is interrupted, do not capitalize the first letter of the continuation.

"**M**y nose," the princess cried, "**h**as grown too long."

Proper Nouns and Adjectives

Capitalize proper nouns and adjectives derived from proper nouns.

Sherwood Forest; Robin Hood; English flag

Titles

Capitalize titles that precede a name. Do not capitalize titles that are not used with a name.

In 1952 *Queen Elizabeth II* became the *queen* of England.

Capitalize titles that substitute for a name in a noun of direct address.

"Can you clean his wound, *Doctor*?"

Do not capitalize family members unless used as a substitute for a name or with a name.

He succeeded his *father* as king.

Did *Father* say that we could play outside?

An exception is *sir* or *madam* as a noun of direct address: "Stand back, sir," demanded Robin.

Calendar Words

Capitalize days of the week and months of the year. Do not capitalize seasons: spring, summer, fall, winter.

Timmy enjoyed peas on a hot *summer Wednesday* evening in *June*.

Directions

Capitalize compass directions when they refer to a region or proper name. Do not capitalize these words when they indicate direction. Do not capitalize words like *northward* or *northern*.

On her journey *north* Eden encountered few obstacles.
Eden is heading in a *northward* direction but not traveling to a region known as the *North*.

Literary Titles and Subtitles

Capitalize the first word and the last word of titles and subtitles. Capitalize all other words except articles, coordinating conjunctions, and prepositions.

A young girl recited "Mary Had a Little Lamb."

Read *Mozart: The Wonder Boy* by next week.

Numbers

Words

Spell out numbers that can be expressed in one or two words.

twenty; fifty-three; three hundred

Dorinda had racked up *one thousand* text messages on her cell phone in one month.

Spell out ordinal numbers.

first, second, third

The next year the *second* sister was permitted to rise to the surface.

Numerals

Use numerals for numbers that use three or more words.

123; 204

That evening 250 rockets rose in the air.

Never begin a sentence with a numeral.

1492 is a famous year in history. (incorrect)

The year 1492 is a famous year in history. (correct)

Use numerals with dates. Do not include *st, nd, rd,* or *th.*

December 25, not December 25th

Meet me at the Green Chapel in one year and one day on January 1, 1400.

Use numerals when numbers are mixed with symbols.

We received $500 in donations last month.

We can expect at least 40% of those invited to attend.

Homophones and Usage

Homophones

Homophones are words that sound alike but are spelled differently and have different meanings.

there *There* is an adverb pointing to a place or point: *over there* (there is the spot).
their *Their* is a possessive pronoun: *their house* (the house belongs to them).
they're *They're* is a contraction: *they're finished* (they are finished).

Although less common, *there* can function as a noun, pronoun, or adjective.

your *Your* is a possessive pronoun: *your weapon* (the weapon belongs to you).
you're *You're* is a contraction: *you're finished* (you are finished).

to *To* is a preposition or part of an infinitive: *to the left* (preposition); *to rush* (infinitive).
two *Two* is a number: *two women* (2 women).
too *Too* is an adverb meaning also or to an excessive degree: *I'll go too; too far.*

its *Its* is a possessive pronoun: *its wing* (the wing belongs to the bird).
it's *It's* is a contraction: *it's too bad* (it is too bad).

then *Then* is an adverb meaning next or immediately after: *wake and then eat.*
than *Than* is a word used to show a comparison: *Sam is shorter than Bob.*

affect *Affect* is a verb that means to have an influence or to cause:
Dorinda was too self-centered for anyone else to *affect* her deeply.

effect *Effect* is a noun that refers to the result of some action:
Years of indulgence had the obvious *effect* of spoiling Dorinda.

The definitions given for *affect* and *effect* are the most commonly used.

Usage

Usage errors occur when a word is used incorrectly.

between *Between* is a preposition that refers to two items: She stood *between* the (two) trees.
among *Among* is a preposition that refers to three or more items: She walked *among* them.

like *Like* is a preposition that compares a noun to a noun: Waves rose *like* mountains.
as *As* is a subordinating conjunction that compares a noun to an idea (subject + verb).
The waves rose suddenly *as* the storm swelled.
As is a preposition when it means in the role of: They traveled *as* adults.

farther *Farther* refers to measurable distance: I jumped *farther* than I did yesterday.
further *Further* refers to a figurative distance: We want to avoid *further* delays.
Further functions as a verb when it means to promote: He will *further* the agenda.

Use *farthest* like *farther*, *furthest* like *further.*

lie *Lie* is a verb that means to recline or remain: The hen rarely *lies* down.
lay *Lay* is a verb that means to put something down: Daily, the hen *lays* an egg.

The past tense of *lie* is *lay*, which is the same as the present tense of *to lay*.

infinitive	present	past	past participle
to lie	*lie*	*lay*	*lain*
to lay	*lay*	*laid*	*laid*

Present: The hens *lie* down (recline) after they *lay* eggs (put eggs down).

Past: Yesterday the hens *lay* down (reclined) after they *laid* eggs (put eggs down).

Stylistic Techniques

Fix It! stories teach the stylistic techniques of the Institute for Excellence in Writing. Dress-ups are placed within sentences to strengthen vocabulary and add complex sentence structures. Sentence openers are different ways to begin sentences, encouraging sentence variety. Decorations are stylistic devices that embellish prose.

Dress-Ups

Dress-ups are descriptive words, phrases, and clauses that are placed within a sentence.

Three of the dress-ups encourage stronger vocabulary: -ly adverb, strong verb, quality adjective. The other dress-ups encourage more complex sentence structure: *who/which* clause and *www.asia.b* clause.

-ly Adverb Dress-Up

An -ly adverb is an adverb that ends in *-ly*. Adverbs are words that modify verbs, adjectives, or other adverbs. Most often they tell *how* or *when* something is done. The -ly adverb dress-up is used to enhance the meaning of a word. See page G-15.

See a list of -ly adverbs on page G-43.

Notice how the meaning of this sentence changes when different -ly adverbs are added:

She masqueraded as a poor girl.

She *cleverly* masqueraded as a poor girl.

She *arrogantly* masqueraded as a poor girl.

She *deceptively* masqueraded as a poor girl.

Not all words that end in -ly are adverbs. Impostor -ly adverbs are adjectives. If the word ending in -ly describes a noun, it is an adjective and not an adverb.

Adjective Test:

the _______ pen

To find -ly adverbs to use in your writing, use a thesaurus or vocabulary words. Alternatively, look at -ly adverb word lists on the *Portable Walls for Structure and Style Students*® or the IEW Writing Tools App.

Common Impostors
These -ly words are adjectives.

chilly	holy	lovely	queenly
friendly	kingly	lowly	ugly
ghastly	knightly	orderly	worldly
ghostly	lonely	prickly	wrinkly

Strong Verb Dress-Up

A strong verb is an action verb that creates a strong image or feeling. It helps a reader picture what someone or something is doing. See page G-9.

Verb Test:

I ______ .

It ______ .

Challenge students to distinguish between strong verbs and vague ones.

The mermaids often *went* to the castle.
The mermaids often *visited* the castle and *toured* its opulent halls.

The horse *was* in the barn.
The horse *buried* itself in the hay.

The mermaids' hands *were nibbled* on by the fish.
The fish *nibbled* the mermaids' hands.

Quality Adjective Dress-Up

A quality adjective is a descriptive word that provides specific details about a noun or pronoun. Like a strong verb, a quality adjective provides a strong image or feeling. See page G-14.

Adjective Test:

the ______ pen

Notice how the image of *brook* changes with the use of different adjectives. In both examples, the first suggested adjective is weak, whereas the other two provide a stronger image or feeling.

He hurdled the *small* brook.
He hurdled the *narrow* brook.
He hurdled the *babbling* brook.

The *big* stranger greeted Robin.
The *confident* stranger greeted Robin.
The *disagreeable* stranger greeted Robin.

To find strong verbs and quality adjectives to use in your writing, use a thesaurus or vocabulary words. Alternatively, look at word lists on the *Portable Walls for Structure and Style Students* or the IEW Writing Tools App.

Advanced

Deliberate use of dual -ly adverbs, strong verbs, or quality adjectives, especially when the words add a different nuance, enriches prose and challenges students to be precise with words chosen. Classic writers of the past like Charles Dickens and persuasive essayists like Winston Churchill have used duals and triples to convey their meaning most powerfully.

The ship glided away *smoothly* and *lightly* over the tranquil sea.

The wind *filled* and *lifted* the ship's sails.

All who beheld her wondered at her *graceful, swaying* movements.

To punctuate dual adjectives properly, see page G-24.

Who/Which Clause Dress-Up

A *who/which* clause is a dependent clause that provides description or additional information about the noun it follows.

The *who/which* clause immediately follows the noun it describes.

Robin Hood cut a staff, *which measured six feet in length.*
Which measured six feet in length describes the staff.

Frederick hoped to make friends with the princess, *who frequently visited the garden.*
Who frequently visited the garden describes the princess.

A *who/which* clause is a dependent clause that begins with the word *who* or *which.*

Forms of *who* include *whom* and *whose.* See page G-6.

Use *who* when referring to people, personified animals, and pets.
Use *which* when referring to things, animals, and places.

Because the *who/which* clause is a dependent clause, it must be added to a sentence that is already complete. If only the word *who* or *which* is added, a fragment is formed.

The noise alerted Sam. (sentence)
The noise, *which alerted Sam.* (fragment)
The noise alerted Sam, *who drove to safety.* (sentence)
The noise, *which alerted Sam,* alerted him to drive to safety. (sentence)

If the *who/which* clause is removed, a sentence must remain.

Place commas around a *who/which* clause if it is nonessential to the meaning of the sentence.

William**,** *who had little***,** shared with his neighbors. (nonessential, commas)

Do not place commas around a *who/which* clause if it is essential to the meaning of the sentence. See page G-26.

The students *who finished the test* left early. (essential, no commas)
The clause is essential because it defines which students left early.

Although the word *that* may begin an adjective clause, a *that* clause is not a *who/which* clause dress-up.

Advanced

A *who* clause always describes a single noun.

A *which* clause can describe a single noun, or it can describe the entire idea that comes before *which.*

You have killed the king's deer, *which is a capital offense.*
It is not the *deer* (noun before *which* clause) that is the offense but killing it—
the entire idea expressed in the main clause.

If a *who/which* clause contains a *be* verb, the *who* or *which* and the *be* verb can be removed to form an invisible *who/which* clause. An invisible *who/which* clause is called an appositive or appositive phrase, not a clause because the subject (*who* or *which*) and the be verb have been removed from the written sentence. Follow the same comma rules.

Dorinda frustrated Lady Constance, ~~who was~~ her companion since childhood.

All had come to Sherwood Forest, ~~which was~~ a vast, uncharted wood.

www.asia.b Clause Dress-Up

A *www.asia.b* clause is a dependent clause that usually functions as an adverb. It begins with a subordinating conjunction (www word) and contains both a subject and a verb.

PATTERN

www word + subject + verb

Robin Hood and his band guffawed loudly *until the stranger showed irritation.*
Remain on the other side *while I make a staff.*

There are many subordinating conjunctions. The most common are taught using the acronym *www.asia.b*: when, while, where, as, since, if, although, because. Other words function as subordinating conjunctions: after, before, until, unless, whenever, whereas, than. See page G-13.

Memorize the most common www words using the acronym *www.asia.b:* when, while, where, as, since, if, although, because.

Because the *www.asia.b* clause is a dependent clause, it must be added to a main clause. Although an adverb clause may appear anywhere in a sentence, the *www.asia.b* clause dress-up should not begin a sentence because only sentence openers begin sentences.

Use a comma after an adverb clause that comes before a main clause.
PATTERN AC, MC

That morning *while it rained*, Timmy stayed indoors.

Do not use a comma before an adverb clause.
PATTERN MC AC

Timmy stayed indoors (no comma) *when it rained.*

An adverb clause follows the pattern www word + subject + verb. If a verb is not present, the group of words is likely a prepositional phrase and not an adverb clause.

Dorinda prepared the guestroom *after supper.*
After supper is not a clause because it does not contain a subject and a verb.
After supper is a prepositional phrase.

Dorinda prepared the guestroom *after they ate supper.*
After they ate supper is a clause because it contains both a subject (they) and a verb (ate).

Two tricks help tell the difference between a phrase and a clause.

Look for a verb. A clause must have a verb. A prepositional phrase will not have a verb.

Drop the first word of the phrase or clause in question and look at what is left.

If it is a sentence, the group of words is an adverb clause; if it is not, the words form a prepositional phrase.

~~after~~ supper
This does not have a verb. This does not form a sentence. This is a phrase.

~~after~~ they ate supper
This has a verb (ate). This forms a sentence. This is a clause.

Advanced

When the www words *as, where, when* begin a clause that follows and describes a noun, the clause is probably an adjective clause. Test by inserting *which is* between the noun and www word. If it sounds correct, the clause is an adjective clause, not an adverb clause. Punctuate accordingly. See pages G-21 and G-26.

King Arthur decided to climb to the top of the cliff, *where he could drink from the pool of water.*
King Arthur decided to climb to the top of the cliff, [which is] *where he could drink from the pool of water.*
This is an adjective clause beginning with the word *where*. Because it is nonessential, it requires commas.

When the www words *although, while,* and *whereas* present an extreme contrast to the main clause in the sentence, insert a comma. This is an exception to the more common rule **MC AC.** See page G-26.

Timmy favored the country, *while* Johnny preferred the city.

Advanced Dress-Ups

Dual -ly Adverbs, Strong Verbs, Quality Adjectives

Deliberate use of dual -ly adverbs, strong verbs, or quality adjectives, especially when the words add a different nuance, enriches prose and challenges students to be precise with words chosen. Classic writers of the past like Charles Dickens and persuasive essayists like Winston Churchill have used duals and triples to convey their meaning most powerfully.

The ship glided away *smoothly* and *lightly* over the tranquil sea.
The wind *filled* the ship's sails and *propelled* the ship through the sea.
All who beheld her wondered at her *graceful, swaying* movements.

Invisible *Who/Which* Clause

An invisible *who/which* clause is formed when the word *who* or *which* is followed by a *be* verb. Removing *who* or *which* and the *be* verb that follows allows for a more elegant construction. Follow the same comma rules.

Not all *who/which* clauses can be made invisible.

Dorinda frustrated Lady Constance, ~~who was~~ her companion since childhood.

All had come to Sherwood Forest, ~~which was~~ a vast, uncharted wood.

Teeter-Totters

dual
-ly adverbs
www.asia.b
verb

The adverb teeter-totter uses a verb as a fulcrum with dual -ly adverbs preceding the verb and a *www.asia.b* clause following it. Both the -ly adverbs and the *www.asia.b* clause modify the same verb. **PATTERN -ly -ly verb *www.asia.b***

The tortoise *slowly* yet *steadily* finished the race *as the crowd watched in awe.*

dual
adjectives
w/w clause
noun

The adjective teeter-totter uses a noun as a fulcrum with dual quality adjectives preceding the noun and a *who/which* clause following it. Both the quality adjectives and the *who/which* clause describe the same noun. **PATTERN adjective adjective noun *w/w***

The Little Mermaid placed the prince on the *fine white* sand, *which the sun had warmed.*

Noun Clause

A noun clause dress-up is a dependent clause that functions as a noun and begins with the word *that.* It typically follows a verb and answers the question *what.*

If the *that* clause is an adjective clause and not a noun clause, the word *which* can replace *that.*

The king of the beasts never imagined *that* a puny rodent could help him.
The king of the beasts never imagined *which* a puny rodent could help him.
This does not make sense. This is not an adjective clause but a noun clause.

The king of the beasts was freed from a net *that* a mouse had persistently gnawed.
The king of the beasts was freed from a net *which* a mouse had persistently gnawed.
This makes sense. This is an adjective clause. See page G-21.

An invisible noun clause occurs when the word *that* is implied, not stated directly.

Dorinda never seemed to understand [that] *she was responsible.*

Frederick could tell [that] *he would relish his palace stay.*

Noun clauses do not take commas.

People felt (no comma) *that Robin Hood was like them.*

Robin Hood was pleased (no comma) *that he had escaped.*

Sentence Openers

Sentence openers are descriptive words, phrases, and clauses that are added to the beginning of a sentence.

There are six openers—six ways to open or begin a sentence. Using various sentence openers forces sentence variety, which will improve writing quality. Learning the sentence opener patterns and their related comma rules will result in sophisticated writing skills.

#1 Subject Opener

A subject opener is simply a sentence that begins with its subject. This is the kind of sentence one most naturally writes. A subject opener begins with the subject of the sentence.

Fish glide among the branches.

There may be an article or adjectives in front of the subject, but that does not change the sentence structure. It is still a #1 subject opener.

The colorful fish glide among the branches.

#2 Prepositional Opener

A prepositional opener is a prepositional phrase placed at the beginning of a sentence. See pages G-8 and G-18.

If a prepositional opener has five words or more, follow it with a comma.

Under the table (no comma) the tiny mouse hid.

*Under the heavy wooden table***,** the tiny mouse hid.

If two or more prepositional phrases open a sentence, follow the last phrase with a comma.

*Under the heavy wooden table in the kitchen***,** the tiny mouse hid.

If a prepositional opener functions as a transition, follow it with a comma.

*In fact***,** the cook was afraid of mice.

If a prepositional opener is followed by a main clause that has the verb before the subject, do not use a comma.

Under the heavy wooden table hid a tiny mouse.

PATTERN

preposition + noun (no verb)

Because of begins prepositional phrases.

Because begins clauses.

Advanced

An invisible prepositional opener is formed when some kind of time is followed by the main clause. The preposition *on* or *during* is implied.

~~On~~ *Wednesday* we will go to the beach.

~~On~~ *The day before yesterday* we visited the park.

~~During~~ *That afternoon* she visited friends.

#3 -ly Adverb Opener

An -ly adverb opener is an -ly adverb placed at the beginning of a sentence. Beginning the sentence with an -ly adverb changes the rhythm of the sentence.

Test:

It was ____ that ____.

Use a comma if an -ly adverb opener modifies the sentence.

Foolishly, Timmy bit into a hot pepper.
Test: It was foolish that Timmy bit ... makes sense.
Foolishly modifies the sentence. A comma is required.

Do not use a comma if an -ly adverb opener modifies the verb.

Eagerly Timmy ate a ripe cucumber.
Test: It was eager that Timmy ate a ripe cucumber ... does not make sense. *Eagerly* modifies the verb *ate*. A comma is not needed.

Advanced

In some cases, the comma indicates the meaning of the sentence.

Sorrowfully Timmy acceded to the counsel of Johnny.
He acceded, but he did so sorrowfully, with regret.

Sorrowfully, Timmy acceded to the counsel of Johnny.
This opener indicates that Timmy made a mistake in acceding to Johnny's advice.
It is sorrowful that Timmy acceded to his Johnny's counsel.

-ly Adverbs List

angrily
annoyingly
boredly
busily
commonly
completely
constantly
continuously
critically
deceptively
disappointingly
discouragingly
excitedly
finally
greedily
happily
historically
hopefully
horribly
joyfully
kindly
meanly
miraculously
mostly
mournfully
oddly
proudly
rapidly
repeatedly
sadly
seriously
shamefully
sleepily
slyly
sneakily
strangely
suddenly
tragically
uncomfortably
unexpectedly
unhappily
usually
viciously
vigorously
violently
warmly
willfully
wisely

#4 -ing Opener

An -ing opener is a participial phrase placed at the beginning of a sentence.

A #4 -ing opener is a participial opener.

Taking up his bow, Robin Hood shot with unparalleled skill.

PATTERN -ing word/phrase, main clause. This is the most sophisticated sentence pattern. It is easily written when the pattern is followed. The sentence must begin with an action word that ends in -ing. This is called a participle. The -ing word/phrase and comma are followed by a main clause. The thing (subject of main clause) after the comma must be the thing doing the inging.

The thing after the comma must be the thing doing the inging.

Gathering their three gifts, the soldiers visited a neighboring king. The sentence begins with an action word that ends in -ing: *Gathering*
The -ing word/phrase and comma are followed by a main clause: *the soldiers visited a neighboring king.*
The thing (subejct of main clause) after the comma must be the thing doing the inging: *soldiers* (subject) *are gathering.*

An illegal #4 opener is grammatically incorrect. If the thing after the comma is not the thing doing the inging, the sentence does not make sense. This is known as a dangling modifier.

Hopping quickly, Dorinda let the frog follow her to the dining hall.
Who was hopping quickly? *Dorinda.* This is incorrect because the frog was hopping quickly.

An impostor #4 opener begins with an -ing word but does not follow the pattern. There are two types.

Living at the splendid castle cheered the soldiers.
This is a #1 subject opener. There is neither a comma nor a subject doing the inging. *Living* is the subject.

During the dance she twirled him around.
This is a #2 prepositional opener. *She* (the subject) is not doing the *during.*

Prepositions ending in -ing include *concerning, according to, regarding, during.*

Advanced

An invisible -ing opener is formed when *being* is implied before the first word of the sentence. Removing the word *being* allows for a more elegant construction. Follow the same comma rules.

~~Being~~ Quick-witted and agile, Robert compensated for his limitation with an eagerness to please.

~~Being~~ Relaxed and untroubled, the stranger genially waited for him.

~~Being~~ Encouraged by Samuel's speech, William stepped onto the stage.

#5 Clausal Opener

A clausal opener is an adverb clause placed at the beginning of a sentence. This opener is the same as the *www.asia.b* dress-up. The only difference is placement in the sentence. The opener begins a sentence.

PATTERN AC, MC Use a comma after an adverb clause opener.

If possessions were plundered, Robin and his men would recapture the goods and return them to the poor.

As he approached, Robin Hood noticed a tall stranger on the other side of the stream.

When Robin attempted to cross the river, the stranger blocked his way.

PATTERN

www word + subject + verb

Because begins clauses.

Because of begins prepositional phrases.

An adverb clause follows the pattern www word + subject + verb. If a verb is not present, the group of words is likely a prepositional phrase and not an adverb clause.

After supper, Dorinda prepared the guestroom.
After supper is not a clause because it does not contain a subject and a verb.
After supper is a prepositional phrase.

After they ate supper, Dorinda prepared the guestroom.
After they ate supper is a clause because it contains both a subject (they) and a verb (ate).

Two tricks help tell the difference between a phrase and a clause.

Look for a verb. A clause must have a verb. A prepositional phrase will not have a verb.

Drop the first word of the phrase or clause in question and look at what is left. If it is a sentence, the group of words is an adverb clause; if it is not, the words form a prepositional phrase.

~~After~~ supper
This does not have a verb. This does not form a sentence. This is a phrase.

~~After~~ they ate supper
This has a verb (ate). This forms a sentence. This is a clause.

#6 Vss Opener

A very short sentence (vss) is simply a short sentence. It must be short (two to five words), and it must be a sentence (subject + verb and be able to stand alone). It is not a fragment.

Remember that variety in sentence structure is important in good writing. Purposefully adding a very short sentence can help break up the pattern of sentences in a stylish way. It catches the reader's attention. As a result, place it in a spot that needs emphasis.

Robin Hood left.

The blow inflamed him.

King Morton esteemed values.

As an added challenge, include a strong verb so that the very short sentence packs a punch.

Advanced Sentence Openers

#F Fragment Opener

A fragment that does not leave the reader hanging and that fits the flow of the paragraph can be dramatic and effective. This opener is often used in fictional writing.

Timmy saw his dear friend. (sentence)

Greeting him kindly. (unacceptable fragment)

"Hello, Johnny!" (acceptable fragment)

#Q Question Opener

A question is a complete sentence. It must contain a subject and a verb and make sense.

Where could he take a nap?

#T Transitional Opener

The transitional opener may be an interjection or a transitional word or phrase.

Place commas after a transitional expression.

Meanwhile, Robin's men rested near the river.

Of course, Dorinda and Maribella lived in the castle.

When an interjection expresses a strong emotion, use an exclamation mark. When an interjection does not express a strong emotion, use a comma.

Help! My golden ball has vanished.

Oh, I see it now.

List of Common Transitions

however	first
therefore	next
then	also
thus	moreover
later	hence
now	furthermore
otherwise	henceforth
indeed	likewise

Decorations

Used sparingly, as an artist might add a splash of bright color to a nature painting, these stylistic techniques daringly or delicately decorate one's prose.

Alliteration Decoration

Alliteration is using three or more words close together that begin with the same consonant sound. Our ear likes the repetition of sound. The alliterative words may be separated by conjunctions, articles, short pronouns, or prepositions.

> Samuel was *seeking some* shady relief from the *sweltering sun.*
> *Shady* is not part of the alliteration because it does not have the same initial sound as the other *s* words. It is not the letter that matters but the sound. Thus, *celery* and *sound* are alliterative, but *shady* and *sound* are not.

Question Decoration

The question may be a rhetorical question, which means the answer is understood and does not need to be given, or it may be a question that the writer answers soon after asking. If a character in the story asks a question of another character, that is simply conversation. The question decoration is directed towards the reader, causing the reader to stop and think.

> Someone suddenly appeared on the path. *Who was it?* It was Johnny!

Conversation/Quotation Decoration

Conversation appears in narrative writing when characters talk.

> "You're finally here, Johnny!" exclaimed Timmy.

A quotation appears when the writer uses the exact words that someone else has used. A quotation includes a well-known expression, words stated by a famous person, or words found in another source. When a quotation is used as a decoration, it does not require a citation, but the source should be included as a lead-in. Punctuate correctly. See page G-27.

> As Mark Twain noted, "History may not repeat itself, but it sure does rhyme."

3sss Decoration

3sss stands for three short staccato sentences. The 3sss is simply three #6 very short sentences in a row. Using short sentences together, especially among longer sentences, can be a powerful stylistic technique because the short sentences will draw attention to themselves.

A 3sss will have the most impact when the number of words in each of the sentences is the same or decreasing. Increasing patterns have less impact.

> 4:3:2 Killer bees invaded America. Viciously they attacked. Humans suffered.
>
> 3:3:3 Savage bees attacked. Violently they killed. Nobody was spared.
>
> 2:2:2 Bees invaded. They marauded. Humans perished.

Simile/Metaphor Decoration

Both a simile and a metaphor are figures of speech which compare two items that are very different from each other. The well-known simile *her cheeks are like roses* compares cheeks to roses, two very different things. A simile makes the comparison by using the words *like* or *as*. A metaphor does not use *like* or *as*. It simply refers to one thing as if it is another.

The key to recognizing these figures of speech is that they compare unlike things. For example, to say that a cat is like a tiger is a comparison but not a simile.

The ship dove like a swan between them. (simile)

The waves rose mountains high. (metaphor)

Dramatic Open-Close Decoration

The vss open-close decoration frames a single paragraph. The vss open-close decoration contains two very short sentences two to five words long. One is placed at the beginning of the paragraph, and the other is placed at the end.

Hungry flames roared. (vss open) The farm lay in ashes. (vss close)

Peter sighed. (vss open) Peter had an idea. (vss close)

The mystery was solved! (vss open) The truth was told. (vss close)

The anecdotal open-close decoration frames a composition or essay that includes an introduction and conclusion. An anecdote is a very short story meant to amuse or teach. To use this decoration, begin the introduction with a story to draw in the reader. Revisit the story somewhere in the conclusion.

Anecdotal open (beginning of introduction):

With a bushel of cranberries slung over her shoulder, eight-year-old Jennie Camillo trod through the cranberry bog toward the bushel man who would collect her load. When the infamous photographer Lewis Hine asked her to stop so he could take a picture, she stopped for a brief moment to humor the man. Concernedly Jennie glanced toward her toiling father, who was regarding her stop with annoyance.

Anecdotal close (in the conclusion):

Working during the harvest season, Jennie missed the first six weeks of school. Due to her family's financial struggles, the Camillos were forced to take the whole family to Theodore Budd's bog near Philadelphia before returning home to New Jersey after the harvest.

Triple Extensions

Classic writers of the past have used duals and triples to convey their meaning most powerfully. The trick is to remember "thrice, never twice."

Repeating Words (same word)

Fearing for his sheep, *fearing* that the villagers would not arrive in time, and ultimately *fearing* for his own life, Peter screamed, "Help!" as he bolted down the hill.

Never in the field of conflict was *so* much owed by *so* many to *so* few (Churchill).

Villainy is *the matter*; baseness is *the matter*; deception, fraud, conspiracy are *the matter* (Dickens).

With a *common* origin, a *common* literature, a *common* religion and *common* drinks, what is longer needful to the cementing of the two nations together in a permanent bond of brotherhood (Mark Twain)?

Repeating Clauses

They lived in a land *where* the winter was harsh, *where* food became scarce, and *where* provisions had to be stored.

Repeating Prepositional Phrases

We have not journeyed all this way *across* the centuries, *across* the oceans, *across* the mountains, *across* the prairies, because we are made of sugar candy (Churchill).

Repeating -ings

Gnawing, jerking, and *yanking,* the mouse freed the lion from the thick rope.

The Little Mermaid could be seen *holding* the prince while *kissing* his brow and *stroking* his hair.

Repeating -ly Adverbs

Robin Hood *cheerfully, boldly,* and *fearlessly* led his men.

The mouse *vigorously* gnawed at the tough fibers and *tenaciously* jerked at the rope while he *continuously* assured the lion of escape.

Repeating Adjectives

The *patient, persistent,* and *personable* tortoise determined that at least he would have a chance.

Repeating Nouns

Peter's deceptive cries for help finally determined the *attitude, behavior,* and *actions* of the village people.

Repeating Verbs

With all his might, the mouse *gnawed, jerked,* and *yanked* at the thick rope.